The
Pastoral Care
Case

The Pastoral Care Case

Learning about Care in Congregations

Donald Capps

Gene Fowler

Chalice Press®

St. Louis, Missouri

Biblical quotations, unless otherwise noted, are from the *New Revised Standard Version Bible*, copyright 1989, Division of Christian Education of the National Council of Churches of Christ in the United States of America. Used by permission. All rights reserved.

Cover design: Ross Sherman
Interior design: Elizabeth Wright
Art direction: Elizabeth Wright

This book is printed on acid-free, recycled paper.

Visit Chalice Press on the World Wide Web at
www.chalicepress.com

10 9 8 7 6 5 4 3 2 1   01 02 03 04 05 06

Library of Congress Cataloging–in–Publication Data

Capps, Donald.
    The pastoral care case : learning about care in congregations / Donald Capps, Gene Fowler.
       p.   cm.
    Includes bibliographical references and index.
    ISBN 0-8272-2964-x
    1. Pastoral theology–Study and teaching 2. Pastoral psychology–Study and teaching. 3. Pastoral counseling–Study and teaching. 4. Case method.
I. Fowler, Gene, 1952–   II. Title.
    BV4012   .C318   2001
253' .07'22–dc21   00-011577

In dedication to
Amy Fowler and Thomas Fowler

Contents

Introduction

Pastoral care in congregations is a ministry of the church that challenges pastors and church members alike to reach out beyond themselves and respond to those who suffer. For many years, pastoral care education has provided students with a means of studying the pastoral care that they provide in order to learn this ministry and to improve their practice of it. In this educational practice, students write cases about their pastoral care and interpret them, most often in the context of a small group or class. We affirm the educational practice of case writing but also believe that it has some serious shortcomings with regard to the congregational setting. Learning pastoral care in the congregational setting today requires a far more intentional focus on the congregation than was acknowledged in the twentieth century.

Originally, case writing for learning pastoral care was used in clinical settings, mostly hospitals, and was part of the case method of teaching used in clinical pastoral training, or what is known today as clinical pastoral education. In the mid-twentieth century, the influence of clinical pastoral training was felt in seminaries and divinity schools, and as a result students began writing cases about their pastoral care in the congregational setting. One problem accompanying this shift from the clinical to the congregational setting, with regard to case writing, was that the practice was designed for use in clinical settings. This meant that the only aspects of pastoral care in congregations that could be studied were those closely resembling pastoral care as it occurred in clinical settings. Differences between the clinical and congregational settings were minimized to such an extent that many facets of pastoral care in congregations were simply ignored.

We believe that pastors should be able to tell the story of the pastoral care they practice in all its diversity and complexity, no matter how different it is from that found in other settings, such as pastoral counseling centers. Accordingly, in this book, we are providing a new case model designed from within the congregational setting and intended for use in that setting. This model is more than just another case outline. It includes a new way of understanding cases in pastoral care education, and it gives pastors the flexibility they need to write about what they actually are experiencing in pastoral care. Masters of Divinity students and Doctor of Ministry students can use this case model for writing about the pastoral care they practice in the congregational setting and for studying that care in order to increase the effectiveness of their pastoral care ministry.

Of course, not every student is headed for pastoral ministry. Some are concerned with specialized ministry, such as pastoral psychotherapy or chaplaincy. Does this book have relevance for them? We believe that it does, not in the sense of denying differences between the ministry settings, but instead in the sense of acknowledging differences and similarities and learning from them. It is no longer possible to view pastoral care globally as if it were the same in all institutional settings. Nor is it possible to set up clinical settings as the sources of knowledge and skill in pastoral care as if this knowledge and skill could be transferred whole and intact to the congregational setting. This ignores the impact of the setting as a context that helps determine the meaning and practice of the pastoral care occurring within its bounds. Rather, the congregational setting itself must be seen as a primary source of knowledge and skill in pastoral care as it is practiced in that setting.

We have written this book together. Gene Fowler wrote chapters 1 through 4, and Donald Capps wrote chapters 5 and 6 and the epilogue. In the chapters, however, readers will see that we have used *we* instead of *I*, which indicates that we genuinely are together in our views. This has come about through sharing our writings, through mutual critique, through our effort to be open to each other's insights, and through conversation over a long period of time. When *I* is used, it is for a specific reason in the chapter. Another feature of our coauthorship is that Gene Fowler is the pastor of a congregation, and Donald Capps is a professor of pastoral care. Because the subject of this book is about learning pastoral care in congregations through case writing, our two professional orientations have given us a broader outlook than we could have had otherwise.

In chapter 1, the procedure for case interpretation is presented, and it will be used throughout the book. Those who practice pastoral care in congregations can use this procedure when studying their pastoral care or that of others. It will be conveyed through a historical discussion of pastoral care education in the twentieth century. This chapter also explains why a new form of case is needed for studying pastoral care in congregations.

In chapter 2, this new form of case, called the pastoral care case, is presented. Pastors are given a new way to envision the case, as well as a new way to envision their self-understanding as case writers, that fits with their actual ministry of pastoral care in the church. Practical issues associated with case writing are addressed, and a case format for use in congregations is provided.[1]

In chapter 3, the kind of meaning that the pastoral care case discloses is presented. Case meaning cannot be discerned except through case interpretation. The two go together, disclosure of meaning and case interpretation. Nevertheless, if case interpreters are going to have any idea of what to expect from interpreting the pastoral care case, the kind of meaning it discloses must be discussed in its own right. It is very important to focus on this meaning, because encountering it is essential for learning through case interpretation.

In chapter 4, the other side of the coin, learning from case interpretation, is presented. The emphasis in this chapter is on showing how interpreting cases of others can help readers improve their own pastoral care in the congregational setting. A pastoral care case is presented, written according to the format found in chapter two, and then is interpreted. This chapter culminates in a discussion of possibilities for learning based on encountering the meaning disclosed through case interpretation.

In chapter 5, the focus shifts from case interpretation to the way that pastoral care case writing contributes to learning. Educationally, there is a distinction between learning from a case written by someone else and learning from one's own case. Although case writers do learn from case interpretation, their learning actually begins much earlier, with the writing itself. A case writer has the problem of needing to become more "at home" in the world of caring ministry, and case writing helps fulfill this need. This chapter includes an extensive case discussion showing how case writing can help the writer grow in self-understanding and in understanding the pastoral care situation about which the case is being written.

---

[1]This chapter is an extensive revision of an article published in *The Journal of Pastoral Care.* See Gene Fowler, "Studying Pastoral Care in Congregations: A Hermeneutical Approach," *The Journal of Pastoral Care* 52, no. 4 (Winter 1998): 323–38.

In chapter 6, a significant limitation of pastoral care case writing is presented. A case in pastoral care education is meant for others to read, normally other students and a teacher. This raises the question of what gets "written out" of cases about pastoral care because of fear of exposure. Most often what gets "written out" are psychological aspects involving the internal world of the case writer. Although there is no perfect antidote, the psychological concept of introspection is presented as a method for case writing that can help case writers include more of themselves in cases.

Pastoral care in congregations happens in a multitude of circumstances, and it may touch the panorama of life from its depths to its heights. Our hope is that pastors of churches will dare to tell their stories of pastoral care and that they and others will learn from those stories in the service of more effective caring ministry to those who suffer.

1

Case Interpretation in Pastoral Care Education

Learning to practice pastoral care in congregations more effectively requires studying the pastoral care that is happening there. One way of studying pastoral care is through cases, and accordingly this chapter will present a procedure essential for learning from pastoral care cases, the procedure for case interpretation. It will be introduced in the first section about the origin of the case method of teaching, and different aspects of case interpretation will be discussed in each succeeding section. In addition, this chapter will show why a new form of case is needed for studying pastoral care in congregations.

Case interpretation is part of the case method of teaching created at the Harvard School of Law in the late nineteenth century. Gradually this innovative educational method proved to be effective for other professions, such as medicine and business. It even played a seminal role in the development of clinical pastoral education, and it continues to be a factor in the education of pastors today when cases are used for studying pastoral care.

The Case Method of Teaching and the Common Law

There are two forms of law in the United States. One form is legislation, and the second form is the English and American common law, also called case law. The written opinion of a judge in the court of appeals constitutes the legal case embodying the common law. The case method of teaching was created as a way to teach this form of law, and the person credited with this creation is Christopher Columbus Langdell, a lawyer who became a Harvard Law School professor in 1869 and dean in 1870. Dr. Joseph Redlich (1914), a law professor from Vienna who reported on the case method of teaching law for the Carnegie Foundation, observed that the case method of teaching was "an entirely original creation of the American mind in the realm of law" (9).

Langdell (1871) brought to Harvard the conviction that the only way to teach and learn law effectively was by examining cases, the original sources of the common law. Out of this conviction, and following reflection on what was needed for successfully teaching law, he decided to gather a series of cases and use them as the texts for his courses rather than textbooks. Not only were the usual legal textbooks replaced with cases but lecturing was replaced with a certain type of conversation between the professor and the students. Langdell would begin his class by having students briefly analyze an assigned case with respect to facts and law contained in it. Next, he would ask a series of questions designed to reveal gradually the entire law discovered from the facts of the case being discussed, and such questions would stimulate doubts, questions, and objections by students, to which he would respond. In this way, he and his students worked together to unfold the legal content in specific cases, thereby enabling the students to learn the principles the common law comprised. Langdell and his students early on described this classroom process as the Socratic method (39).

From this brief description of the Socratic method, it is possible to identify the procedure for case interpretation. It involves two steps: (a) identifying the facts of the case and (b) discovering the principle contained in those facts. These two steps are the backbone of the case interpretation procedure that found its way into pastoral care education through the case method of teaching. This is not the only contribution that the original case method of teaching law has for us, however.

Langdell had to figure out how a large class of students could have adequate access to the cases, and his answer was to create the first legal casebook, *A Selection of Cases on the Law of Contracts*. Redlich observed that, in addition to the creation of a new law school teaching method, the actual ingenious discovery that Langdell made was the "modern case-book" (Redlich, 1914, 59). The more difficult problem, figuring out which cases should be included in the new text, was resolved through creation of a principle designed to be used as the basis for choosing cases. The first part of the principle contained Langdell's understanding of the law as a science, and the second part contained his view of what constituted a true lawyer. The first part of this educational principle is important for understanding how to use the case interpretation procedure, and the second part shows how learning from case interpretation leads to actual practice, so let's turn to the first part.

Law as Science

When he said that law was a science, Langdell meant that the law consisted of principles or doctrines having a history, growing slowly to their present state, sometimes over centuries. These principles were embodied in a series of cases. Because there were relatively few principles in any given area of law, there were correspondingly few cases relevant to a given legal topic such as contracts (vi). He believed there were so few that a casebook could contain all the essential ones.

Langdell came to Harvard at a time when American education was shifting from old classical ideals to a newer theory that made room for the practical disciplines in the university. One important consequence of this shift was that the science laboratory was brought into the university. Such an atmosphere was fertile ground for establishing the view that law was a science and for using that view as the justification for its existence in the university. The president of Harvard at this time, Charles Eliot, was a former scientist who had known Langdell as a law student at Harvard, and it was he who later brought Langdell to teach there. This president welcomed an analogy between law and the physical sciences. The law was to be studied "from its own concrete phenomena, from law cases, in the same way that the laws of the physical sciences are derived from physical phenomena and experiments" (Redlich, 15). Like physical laws, legal principles were to be derived, or learned, inductively from the facts of the case. This educational analogy between law and science said that learning the law involved examining its original sources, the cases, using the inductive method of reasoning, which moved from the particular (facts of the case) to the general (legal principles) as if law were a natural science.

If there is anything that permeates the understanding of case interpretation in pastoral care education, it is precisely this use of inductive reasoning in analogy with scientific method. However, inductive reasoning is only part of scientific method, as Redlich pointed out.

Redlich was not favorably disposed toward the inductive analogy and, consequently, argued that it portrayed a misunderstanding of scientific method. He pointed out that induction does not exhaust scientific method, because deduction also plays an important role in science. Accordingly, when a judge decided a case on the basis of the common law, that judge was not discovering a principle of law inductively. Rather, the judge was applying a preexisting legal norm, or principle, to the case. Therefore, the intellectual activity of the judge was deductive, "for by deduction we mean the application of an already existing general rule to the particular case" (1914, 56–57).

This point, that deductive reasoning plays a role in case interpretation, is very important for understanding case interpretation in pastoral care education. Just as the judge applies a preexisting legal principle to the facts of the case, so pastoral care students apply preexisting pastoral care principles to their cases. Often, what we are calling pastoral care principles take the form of interdisciplinary models involving theology and the social sciences. For instance, depression may be viewed theologically and psychologically, and this interdisciplinary understanding of depression may be brought to bear on a case. Traditionally, the discipline of pastoral theology has involved the theoretical construction of these principles used in the deductive part of case interpretation.

When pastoral care students begin learning principles (models, norms, "general rules") in relation to case interpretation, teachers bring the influence of preexisting pastoral care principles into the interpretive conversation with students. And students themselves bring implicit understandings of care and implicit assumptions about various facets of human life and suffering into case interpretation from their past experience and knowledge. Without a preexisting principle, even if undeveloped and implicit, it is not possible to move from the facts of the case to discernment of the principle as contained in those facts. This is because evaluation of the facts of the case on the basis of the preexisting principles is what allows the principle as contained in the facts to be revealed. Therefore, case interpretation in pastoral care education includes an interplay between deductive and inductive reasoning. Case interpretation is inductive in the sense that it begins with identifying the facts of the case and then moves to a search for the principle contained in the facts of the case. But the second step of discerning the principle contained in the facts of the case requires the deductive evaluation of those facts based on a preexisting pastoral care principle.

Within the case method of teaching, case interpretation provides a certain kind of learning which includes the interplay between inductive and deductive reasoning. It is precisely this interplay that the case interpreter learns to exercise in actual practice, which brings us to the second part of Langdell's educational principle.

The True Lawyer

Determining that law was a science set the stage for Langdell to explain the second part of his educational principle, focusing on what a lawyer does in relation to the law. He argued that the true lawyer is one who masters legal principles in such a way that they can be applied "with constant facility and certainty to the ever-tangled skein of human affairs" (vi). The metaphor "the ever-tangled skein of human affairs" beautifully communicated the conditions under which a lawyer applies the law. Once yarn has been tangled, it becomes very difficult to knit with it. First the yarn must be untangled, and wound into a smooth ball so that it can be pulled evenly. The skein metaphor says that a true lawyer learns to identify tangled behaviors in human events and stories as facts of the case so that they can be evaluated deductively based on a preexisting legal principle. The result was to be that the legal principle as contained in the tangle of particular human affairs could be discerned.

When pastoral care principles are learned, they too are applied with a growing measure of "facility and certainty" in the midst of an "ever-tangled skein of human affairs," or real-life pastoral care situations, not just cases. For instance, let's say that a pastor has learned about the concept of bereavement. Each time the pastor encounters a grieving church member or family, that pastor does not have to learn about the grief process all over again from scratch. Instead, the pastor applies an understanding of bereavement in the midst of an "ever-tangled skein of human affairs," in this instance the life of an individual or family who mourns the loss of someone who was loved. Bereavement as contained in this particular situation is discerned, and in turn it may contribute to the pastor's growing understanding of bereavement.

In this section, the case interpretation procedure has been introduced. It includes identifying the facts of the case and discerning a principle contained in those facts. The way that this procedure is put into practice is through a combination of inductive and deductive reasoning. Finally, this learning gets transferred to actual, real-life situations.

Dr. Richard Cabot was one of the first to draw on this original educational method when he used it for teaching medical diagnosis. We turn now to Cabot because he played a key role in bringing the case method of teaching into pastoral care education (Henri Nouwen, 1977, 12–20).

The Case Method of Teaching Medicine

Some think that the Harvard Graduate School of Business Administration, founded in 1908, was the first educational arena to borrow the case method of teaching law, but this is not true. The first business casebook was published in 1920. But by 1898, Cabot drew on the case method of teaching law for teaching a course in medical diagnosis at Harvard Medical School. For eight years he used and tested written cases in what he called case-teaching exercises, which led to publication of his first medical casebook, *Case Teaching in Medicine* (1906). Five years later, Cabot's two-volume work on diagnosis, *Differential Diagnosis* (1911), was published.

Much as Langdell had done, Cabot explained his case method of teaching medical diagnosis in the introduction of his first casebook (1906). His subject was diagnostic reasoning in relation to physical illness. The facts of the case were symptoms of physical illness instead of legal facts. The principle to be discovered from the facts of the case was disease instead of law, and diagnostic reasoning replaced legal reasoning as the way to get from symptoms to the disease. Keep in mind that whether the reasoning is called "legal" or "diagnostic," it still involves the inductive and deductive reasoning associated with case interpretation. In this regard, the inductive and deductive reasoning involved in pastoral care case interpretation could be called pastoral care reasoning.

Diagnostic reasoning, wrote Cabot, was based on interpreting the data of the case, consisting of the signs of physical illness or the identified symptoms. Because it was possible to collect the data of the medical history and of the physical examination and still not be able to understand what the symptoms meant, the diagnostic reasoning process was extremely important. It enabled the doctor to determine the meaning of the symptoms in relation to a specific disease and thereby form a diagnosis, which then created the possibility of developing a prognosis and treatment plan. The case method of teaching medical diagnosis also included Cabot's version of the Socratic method of classroom case discussion revised to fit the needs of the medical topic (vii–x).

Cabot had been using the case method of teaching for more than twenty years when he became involved with those who pioneered the clinical training of seminary students. Now the case method of teaching goes through its second transfer, from medical education to clinical pastoral training.

The Case Method of Teaching in Clinical Pastoral Training

The inauguration of clinical pastoral training, what today is called clinical pastoral education, is attributed to Anton Boisen, the first full-time psychiatric hospital chaplain in the United States. In his book *The Exploration of the Inner World* (1936) Boisen wrote, "Almost from the beginning of the specialized religious ministration to the mentally ill, upon which I have been engaged during the last twelve years, I have been concerned in a plan for the clinical training of theological students" (250). This plan for clinical training came to fruition in the summer of 1925, when four seminary students became the first group to participate in clinical pastoral training at Worcester State Hospital with Boisen.

Boisen described what it was about the mentally ill that caused him to prefer the psychiatric setting for clinical training:

> In the case of the mental sufferer...nothing can be taken for granted. His inner world has gone to pieces or it has been twisted out of shape. The culture patterns in which he was brought up no longer hold good and he questions everything. In so far, therefore, as we are to begin with his experiences and learn to see through his eyes, we must reexamine the foundations of all religious faith and learn to understand the laws and the forces which are involved in his experience. Herein lies the challenge of this problem to the student of religion...It challenges him to discover in the experiences of his patients the operations of that same power that makes for health which Dr. Cabot has found in the human body. (252)

The story of Boisen and the origin of clinical pastoral training is readily available. What is of immediate concern is the part of this story having to do with the case method of teaching that Boisen used. According to Nouwen (1968), the essential aspect of Boisen's training of theological students was "the presentation and discussion of cases" (59). A major influence on Boisen in this regard was a course taught by Cabot on preparing cases for teaching. This influence, along with other case influences, was brought into clinical pastoral training (Glenn H. Asquith, 1980). Boisen made an original contribution to the case method of teaching by having students write their own cases rather than being confined to reading those prepared by the teacher (Boisen, 1936, 260).

To develop a case format appropriate for studying psychiatric patients, Boisen drew on available models of psychiatric case histories. According to Asquith (1980), a case was to include such information as the social and religious backgrounds of the patient, personal history from childhood to adulthood, and the history and characteristics of the present psychiatric disorder. A case also included sections on diagnosis of the patient's mental illness and interpretation of the patient's experience from a religious standpoint. Asquith suggested that the Boisen case might have been based on a psychiatric form of case created by Adolf Meyer. There were two additional case formats that Boisen used. The first included two sections, one on the religious concerns of the patient and one on religious attitudes and orientation. The second additional format was created with the help of psychiatrist Helen Flanders Dunbar and was used for Boisen's *The Exploration of the Inner World* (89–93).

Rather than drawing on established theological principles and pastoral practices of the church to inform case interpretation, Boisen used his own unique understanding of theology. Asquith says that Boisen viewed theology as a social science in which the focus of study was religious beliefs: "For Boisen, theology is the *study* of religious belief–the 'spiritual forces'–rather than a *statement* of belief itself. In this sense, although theology is the queen of the sciences, it is still a social science that is concerned with religious experience as a biological fact" (1990, 224–25).

Boisen's theology played out in the case method of teaching in a certain way. The facts of the case were various aspects of the psychiatric patient's experience, and the principle to be revealed was religious belief or "spiritual forces" at work in the patient. Nouwen identified diagnosis as the reasoning process that students were supposed to learn in order to move from the patient's experience to this principle. Nouwen saw the diagnostic emphasis in Boisen's case method of teaching as analogous to the diagnostic reasoning process found in Cabot's case method of teaching medical diagnosis (Nouwen, 1968, 58–59). Students were to learn a diagnostic reasoning process that would enable them to gain greater theological understanding of human nature and thereby learn to serve suffering people in their churches more effectively. "We are seeking always to relieve human distress and to train the young minister in the fine art of helping those who are in trouble. We hold that service and understanding go ever hand in hand. Without true understanding there can be no effective service in that which concerns the spiritual life" (Boisen, 1936, 252).

In the final analysis, learning by the case method of teaching is in the service of practice whether that practice is law, medicine, or ministry. Law students could make a natural connection between their case discussions with Langdell and their own future practice of law. Likewise, medical students who studied medical diagnosis with Cabot surely had no trouble making the connection with practicing medicine. However, making the connection between studying mental illness in the psychiatric hospital setting and practicing ministry in the congregational setting necessarily required a far greater leap of imagination by seminary students yet to be ordained.

This history has relevance for contemporary case interpreters because the impact of placing pastoral care education in clinical settings is with us today. Contemporary case interpreters must wrestle with it because differences between institutional settings in pastoral care education and practice in congregational settings no longer can be ignored or downplayed. It cannot be assumed that knowledge or skills can be transferred intact from one setting to another. One indication of difficulty in this regard was present even in Boisen's time. When clinical pastoral training spread to the general hospital, his type of case, based on psychiatric case histories, was abandoned. Although the case method of teaching itself could be transferred, the case format and its content had to be changed. This shift to the general hospital is what generated development of what we know today as the verbatim, of which Boisen did not approve. If shifting pastoral care education merely from one kind of hospital to another required such a significant change, we can assume that shifting to an altogether different setting, such as the congregation, must require at least as much change and even more.

By 1930, clinical pastoral training had gained enough momentum to warrant creation of The Council for the Clinical Training of

Theological Students, Inc. Three years later, the council sent Russell Dicks to Massachusetts General Hospital in Boston to become the chaplain and clinical pastoral training supervisor, replacing Philip Guiles. Now, the setting shifts to clinical pastoral training in the general hospital, where verbatim writing was created. Originally, it was called note-writing.

The Case Method of Teaching and Note-Writing

Before coming to Massachusetts General Hospital in the spring of 1933, Dicks was a student in clinical pastoral training at Worchester State Hospital under the supervision of Carroll Wise, who had studied with Boisen. While at Worchester, Dicks experienced the case method of teaching with the Boisen form of case. However, when he began his chaplaincy and supervisory work in the general hospital setting, he did not find the Boisen psychiatric history form of case appropriate for use in this new setting (Charles E. Hall, 1992, 22–23).

Dicks found himself uncertain about how to study the significant pastoral experience he was observing, and he found himself dissatisfied with his effectiveness as a chaplain. Consequently, he sought a means of transposing his work into a form that could be studied and that could serve as a record of his sickroom visits. Reasoning that what he did was simply talk with patients, he decided to write down as much of the conversations as he could remember. This was so fruitful for his ministry with patients that he soon started sharing his written conversations, which he called notes, with small groups of theological students, asking what they would do in similar circumstances. The resulting questions and discussions caused the students to share his enthusiasm for this process, and soon Dicks required students working under his direction to write notes of their sickroom visits. One student, Rollin Fairbanks, contributed to the evolution of note-writing by leaving a wide left margin, providing Dicks with space to comment on Fairbanks' work. The comments were often questions, and this too became part of the teaching and learning process. Dicks observed that as he studied notes with other students, "those questions were as important as the notes themselves" (1939, 6–8).

Dicks was required to report to Cabot, who was on the staff of Massachusetts General Hospital. Soon they began collaborating on a book titled *The Art of Ministering to the Sick*, which was published in 1936, the same year that Boisen's book was published. In their coauthored book, Cabot and Dicks included a chapter entitled "Note-Writing" that defined and explained the form of case that Dicks had developed. They defined note-writing as "the development on paper of one's work with a given patient after that work is done" (1936, 244). This process provided the opportunity for examining the minister's work with a patient and was the closest thing to an "objective check" on such work that they had yet discovered. Thus, the overall purpose of reproducing a pastoral encounter with a hospital patient was to rethink the encounter and develop its meaning (244).

Cabot and Dicks provided a note-writing outline intended to be suggestive, not an exhaustive straitjacket. The model on which they based this outline came from medical social work, which at that time was a new profession Cabot had helped to establish. The model was a chronological type of recording used in some social service departments when the client and social worker relationship was the most important consideration. The emphasis was on chronology because it was the best way to show how the contact was built up and how psychological developments were taking place in the case. The coauthors argued that, like social workers, pastors sometimes had situations requiring a focus on individuals rather than on social and economic conditions affecting them, hospital ministry being a prime example. Consequently, in these types of situations the minister should discover certain information about patients including their financial condition, family, and so forth, but need not spend time delving into such things as the causes of poverty or other social problems associated with the patient. Thus, the social work model seemed appropriate for note-writing. Below is the outline as written in *The Art of Ministering to the Sick* (255–57). It contains five paragraphs:

1. Name, age, sex, marital status, occupation, family, church membership, physical condition (diagnosis), prognosis.
2. *Reasons for seeing the patient:* how patient came to attention of minister. Problem as described by whoever asked minister to see patient (member of family, patient himself, doctor, nurse, social worker, friend).
3. *First impression:* description and physical appearance. (If minister has not seen patient before, a first impression should be recorded; after that, every time the patient is seen, a new impression should be noted: how was minister received, explanation minister makes to patient, etc.)
4. *What happened:* (At this place should be written the main body of notes. Note whether you directed patient's thought

or whether you simply listened. Show topics patient discussed, citing as many direct quotations as possible, giving worker's questions in direct quotation also.)

5. *Summary:*
    (a) Material revealed, problem as observed, needs of patient.
    (b) How needs can be met, patient's resources, estimated intellectual capacity, attitude toward people, religious beliefs.
    (c) Brief description of patient and of this visit: Did patient seem glad to see you?

Paragraphs one through three introduce the patient and chaplain, including certain aspects of the chaplain's assessment of the situation. Paragraph four contains the word-for-word material and accompanying descriptions that report what happened in the hospital encounter, and paragraph five constitutes an evaluation of the material in the previous paragraphs. In addition to illustrating this format with a note, or case, the coauthors included several additional notes in appendix A of their book. Rather than being called notes, however, they were called histories because they included direct quotations of several pastoral visits with the same patient. Dicks wrote his notes in a narrative form so that the verbatim material and accompanying descriptions sometimes read like short stories.

The main facts of the case in note-writing were direct quotes, the words spoken by the minister and hospital patient during their conversation in the patient's room as written from memory. The principle to be discerned in relation to these facts had three parts. The first part was called the skill of the minister in work with the sick, defined as the way that the minister "conducts himself in the sickroom" (244–45). Such skill, for instance, could be the ability "to discover a mood or an attitude and then to change it" (245). Far and away, the main emphasis of Cabot and Dicks was on discovering the lack of skill and the need to improve it. The second part was called understanding, defined as "a knowledge of people" (247) that the minister brought to the sickroom. This was knowledge gained from past experience, imagination, and spiritual maturity. Skill depended on understanding, but the two were closely interwoven in practice. The third part was called devotion, defined as "one's purpose in seeing a patient" (247). This part of the principle reminded the minister that visiting the sick was more than a social visit.

In clinical pastoral training, students wrote notes and discussed them in groups. Edward Thornton (1970) said that note-writing was "clearly an adaptation" (47) of the Cabot case method of teaching medical diagnosis, which would seem to make sense in the context of clinical pastoral training and given that Cabot was one of the authors. This analogy also would indicate that diagnostic reasoning was to be emphasized. However, in *The Art of Ministering to the Sick*, there was no emphasis on reasoning leading to a diagnosis of the patient. Instead, what was learned about the patient, often put in terms of the patient's need, was seen as part of the information that helped case interpreters to discover and evaluate the skill, understanding, and devotion of the minister in relation to the need of the patient. Thus, while inductive and deductive reasoning processes still moved from the facts of the case to the principle, they should not be labeled diagnostic reasoning because the principle had to do with the chaplain's quality of practice.

Rather, Cabot and Dicks portrayed the note as analogous to the record keeping of medical doctors (including psychiatrists) and of social workers, and they explicitly discussed the note as a type of record. In their examples, they often found the notes to be helpful precisely in the sense of going back over records to discover something that had been overlooked or missed, as a medical doctor might review records. In one illustration, the hospital patient was a Protestant minister who often spoke of becoming a Roman Catholic priest. Although he was married, he never referred to the celibacy of the Roman Catholic priesthood. "He made many references to his daughter but none to his wife. We overlooked this connecting link until three contacts had been reproduced on paper. Then as we studied the notes we became aware of a 'missing wife' and went in search of her" (1936, 250). In studying the three notes, or going over the records, the case interpreters moved from the facts of the case, understood as the words spoken in the conversations between the chaplain and patient, to the part of the principle having to do with the chaplain's skill. In this instance, skill was judged to be lacking in the sense that the chaplain had failed to notice the "missing wife" during visits with the patient. In turn, this discovery was to result in improved skill in the sense that the chaplain now could go "in search of her" during the next visit.

Following the publication of *The Art of Ministering to the Sick*, Dicks wrote the first casebook using notes from chaplaincy, entitled *And Ye Visited Me*, published in 1939. Although Dicks avoided using technical psychiatric language when evaluating cases, he did use psychological resources when interpreting cases in his casebook.

"Much of my interpretation is based upon social work, psychiatric and psychoanalytic insights and techniques which six years of intimate contact with workers in those fields have given me" (11).

The casebook marks an early attempt to take note-writing outside the hospital walls, but even so, the sole focus was still hospital ministry. Making note-writing available to pastors outside the hospital and using psychiatric resources for interpreting notes set the stage for note-writing to be used in new ways. In the future it would be applied to all pastoral care, not just hospital ministry. This meant that it would be used in a new setting, the congregation.

Beyond Hospital Ministry

In the 1940s, there was extensive discussion about the growing relationship between seminary education and clinical pastoral training, including how to nurture this relationship and continue its development (Seward Hiltner, 1945). Teaching courses as part of a theological curriculum was part of this larger issue. According to Charles Gerkin, "by the latter half of the decade of the 1940s one by one the mainline Protestant seminaries in America began to establish departments of pastoral care or pastoral theology rooted in the developments that were taking place in the clinical centers" (1997, 67). Corresponding to this new classroom setting, the focus on the ministry of care began to shift from clinical locations to the congregation.

It might seem natural that shifting the educational focus to pastoral care in the congregational setting would give rise to a new form of case suitable for that setting. After all, just a shift from the psychiatric hospital to the general hospital resulted in replacing the Boisen psychiatric forms of case with note-writing, or the verbatim. Instead, something happened that still affects case interpreters in pastoral care education today. Note-writing was transferred from the general hospital setting to the congregational setting and became the most commonly used form of case for studying pastoral care in congregations during the second half of the twentieth century. Note-writing terminology, however, did not survive. During the 1940s, the terms *report* and *verbatim report* were used often, and during the second half of the century *verbatim* became the standard name used for the Dicks form of case.

Using verbatims for studying pastoral care in congregations had a profound impact on the understanding of this ministry because now it was to resemble chaplaincy. Just as the facts of the case in hospital chaplaincy consisted of the words spoken between the chaplain and patient written from memory, so the facts of the case in pastoral ministry were to be the words spoken between the minister and church member written from memory. Likewise, the principle associated with the facts of the case in the congregational setting would have to be the minister's skill, understanding, and devotion seen in relation to the need of the church member receiving pastoral care. This three-part principle came to be called simply "method," which remains in force today, though the types of methods have changed.

Given that note-writing was being used in a new setting, there were bound to be changes associated with case writing based on differences between hospital chaplaincy and pastoral care in the congregational setting. There were three changes during the 1940s and 1950s that had a lasting impact on pastoral care education. The first one involved the facts of the case. The second change involved the principle associated with the facts of the case, and the third involved pastoral theology. In the next three sections, these changes will be addressed because they all bear on learning from studying pastoral care in congregations.

Verbatim Writing in Congregations: Changing the Facts of the Case

It may seem to many as if the phrase *pastoral care and counseling* sprang full-blown into existence, immediately replacing the historic phrase the *cure of souls*. In reality, there were decades between the demise of the *cure of souls* during the early part of the twentieth century and the emergence of *pastoral care and counseling* in the second half of that century. For example, Boisen reported being taken to task for using the phrase *cure of souls,* so he substituted the phrase *spiritual healing* (1936, 238). Nor did Cabot and Dicks use the *cure of souls*. Instead, they used descriptive phrases such as "the minister goes to the sickroom." What the minister did there was "work with the sick" (1936, 20 and 196). During the late nineteenth and early twentieth centuries, *work* could refer to the ministry of the pastor and also to the ministry of the congregation, seen for instance in Washington Gladden's *The Christian Pastor and the Working Church* (1898). Cabot and Dicks used the term *work* more narrowly to mean what was done in the minister's visit with the hospital patient (1936, 197).

The phrase *pastoral work* became the primary name for the ministry of care in the congregational setting during the second half of the 1940s and the early 1950s. This came about because Dicks transferred *work* from the hospital to the congregation and defined it as ministry with individuals. This included all care conversation between the pastor and church member and encompassed couples and families. In addition, *work* became paired with a related trend that had been developing during the 1940s called pastoral counseling. When *work* and *counseling* were brought together, the original form of what is known today as *pastoral care and counseling* was born. The book in which these two terms were brought together and made into a comprehensive model for ministers to use in their congregations was Dicks's *Pastoral Work and Personal Counseling* (1944). Through this book, Dicks in effect became the architect of the pastoral care and counseling model.

Dicks brought his pioneering experience as a hospital chaplain and clinical pastoral training supervisor to bear on pastoral work in the congregational setting. From a religious standpoint, he saw pastoral work as a spiritual task: "The clergyman's task in pastoral work is to assist spiritual forces at work within the individual..." for the relief of suffering and for spiritual growth (1944, 5–6). At the same time, he argued strongly that pastoral work must be informed by psychology based on the psychiatry of his day. Pastoral work, he said, "takes on new meaning in the light of modern psychology" (3). Ministers were criticized severely for being slow to accept this "coming of light" and for being slow to "awaken" to their pastoral task of caring with the help of psychology (4).

Pastoral work was to happen in two ways, according to Dicks. The first and most prevalent way was through the minister's calling on a church member in the home, at a hospital, at the church member's place of work, on a street corner, or over the phone. The contact could be anywhere (23). Calling was to be the very heart of pastoral ministry. The clinically trained, chaplainlike minister was to ring doorbells daily and always be prepared to offer care. Calling and pastoral care were linked so closely that for all practical purposes they became synonymous. The second form of pastoral work was to be personal, or pastoral, counseling, for which the church member came to the minister's office (vii). Dicks nearly always discussed pastoral work inclusive of both forms, because both focused on the individual and made use of psychology. He distinguished between them by identifying the types of situations addressed when the minister made a call and when the church member came to the minister's office.

After World War II ended and the cold war began, Dicks produced a revised edition of *Pastoral Work and Personal Counseling*, appropriating a new terminology emerging for the ministry of care, called pastoral care, and incorporating it into his model. The appearance of a new journal in 1947, named *The Journal of Pastoral Care,* seems to have provided one of the main influences in the gradual mid-century shift from pastoral work to pastoral care terminology. Dicks (1949) wrote, "Pastoral care is as old as religion. It means ministry to individuals. In its traditional sense it means shepherding of souls, or cure of souls" (vii).

Following the 1944 publication of the first edition of *Pastoral Work and Personal Counseling,* others in the field appropriated the Dicks model, and it became widespread. For instance, Hiltner used it in *Pastoral Counseling* (1949), and Paul Johnson used it in *Psychology of Pastoral Care* (1953). Carroll Wise (1951) practically quoted from Dicks's chapter titles when he described the main difference between care and counseling: "The essential difference between calling and the counseling situation is that in the former the pastor goes to the person while in the latter the person comes to the pastor" (170).

In accord with Dicks's shift in focus from the hospital to the congregation, verbatim writing was taken in a new direction. Now it was to be used for studying pastoral work, the pastor's calling and counseling in the congregational setting. In this new setting, the facts of the case, or the words spoken between the pastor and church member as written from memory, underwent two types of expansion. First, the facts of the case had to represent a multitude of care situations involving individuals, couples, or families in the congregation that often had nothing to do with illness, because the setting was not the hospital. Second, now that pastoral work was divided into two types, calling and counseling, the facts of the case also were split into two types, those associated with calling and those associated with counseling.

Although the facts of the case now could be very diverse, there was only one type of principle to be discovered in relationship to them, that of method. Not even the practical distinction between calling and counseling brought any distinctions between principles or kinds of method. But this changed in 1949 and became more complicated when Hiltner's *Pastoral Counseling* was published.

Verbatim Writing in Congregations: Changing the Principle of the Case

Like Dicks, Hiltner went through clinical pastoral training. According to Hall, "It was Boisen who told Hiltner about clinical training...As a result of Boisen's suggestion, Hiltner entered the clinical training program at Mayview Hospital just outside of Pittsburgh, Pennsylvania, in the summer of 1932 with Donald Beatty as supervisor. The following summer, he was at...Worcester" (1992, 29).

By the 1940s, Hiltner had made the transition from the Boisen form of case to the Dicks form of case and began to use it for teaching pastoral counseling in the seminary context. In *Pastoral Counseling,* Hiltner discussed the case method of teaching pastoral counseling in the congregational setting.[1] Though he did use the term *report,* Hiltner primarily called note-writing an interview, which was case terminology being used by social workers and by psychotherapist Carl Rogers. Pastoral work, in its form of calling, along with the rest of ministry, was viewed solely from the standpoint of how it could lead to pastoral counseling.

In the case method of teaching pastoral counseling used by Hiltner, the facts of the case still involved the words spoken by the minister and church member as written from the case writer's memory. However, the principle to be discovered in relation to the facts of the case was expanded to include two principles. Hiltner followed Dicks by retaining the principle of method, seen in chapter two of *Pastoral Counseling.* In chapter three, he added a Boisen type of principle involving dynamic psychology, so both method and psychological dynamics could be derived from the same facts of the case. In an autobiographical article, Hiltner described how he brought the Boisen and Dicks principles together in the Dicks form of case:

> From Boisen I acquired the bent toward understanding dynamics and maintaining a theological perspective at all

---

[1]John W. Drakeford pointed out in "Ways to Learn Pastoral Counseling," in *An Introduction to Pastoral Counseling,* ed. Wayne E. Oates (Nashville: Broadman Press, 1959), 189, that the educational exercise Hiltner described in chapter two of *Pastoral Counseling* initially was set forth by William U. Snyder in *Casebook of Non-Directive Counseling* (Boston: Houghton Mifflin, 1947).

times although learning everything possible from cognate disciplines. From Dicks I took sensitivity to actual encounters, ways of examining method and technique, and the knowledge that the study of actual conversations is as revelatory about the pastor as about the parishioner. I first combined all these factors in teaching at Union and Yale, then wrote about it in *Pastoral Counseling.* (1980, 92)

Hiltner stopped short of adding a potential third principle to address what happens in the counseling relationship over time, though he did use excerpts from interviews as illustrations when discussing brief and extended pastoral counseling (1949, 80–94). He did not believe the interview could reveal anything about the time dimension of counseling, but he considered only single interviews. A single interview, he said, was like the cross section of a tree. In contrast, studying the time dimension of counseling was like looking at the tree in all its height (1949, 34, 80). It is puzzling that he failed to take a series of interviews into account as a way of studying the time dimension of counseling, especially since both Dicks and Rogers found value in such series. By confining himself to single interviews, Hiltner effectively abandoned the analogy with medical record keeping. Instead, he emphasized teaching seminary students how to make psychotherapeutic responses according to his Rogerian oriented pastoral counseling method, which he called the eductive method.

Note-writing was to undergo yet another transfer, but not to a new setting. It was to play a role in modern pastoral theology.

Verbatim Writing in Pastoral Theology

In *Preface to Pastoral Theology* (1958), Hiltner introduced pastoral theology as a formal theological discipline. The pastoral theologian was to examine ministry, or what Hiltner called "all the operations and functions of the church and minister" (1958, 20), from a certain perspective called shepherding. From reflection on what was discovered through the examination, theological conclusions were to be derived. Engaging in pastoral theology could require many elements, such as the defining and explaining of concepts, dialogue between faith and culture, and interpretation of cases. Hiltner summed it up this way: "Pastoral theology...begins with theological questions and concludes with theological answers, in the interim examining all acts and operations of pastor and church to the degree that they involve the perspective of Christian shepherding" (24).

In pastoral theology, shepherding replaced the fledgling pastoral care terminology, though it was not confined to ministry through calling or counseling. This change was part of a new model of ministry called the perspectival view, in which pastoral ministry was conceived in terms of three perspectives: shepherding persons; communicating the gospel; and organizing the fellowship, or congregation. As a perspective, shepherding involved the pastor's attitude of "tender and solicitous concern" seen in relation to a church member in need who had some readiness to receive help. Hiltner divided shepherding into what he called subgroups consisting of healing, sustaining, and guiding. Healing meant "binding up wounds" in the sense of the good Samaritan parable. Sustaining meant comforting in the sense of "standing by" a person when healing was not possible presently, such as during bereavement. Guiding meant helping a person find a "path" or direction, especially regarding moral and spiritual matters (16–18, 69).

Cases in pastoral theology were to provide the means of examining "all the operations and functions" of the minister and church from the shepherding perspective and were therefore essential for putting pastoral theology into practice. In his use of cases, Hiltner made some questionable choices, however. The most extensive case on which he drew was not from the contemporary ministry of his day. Instead, he opted for a book published in the mid-nineteenth century containing quotes from conversations between a pastor and individuals and families, and he treated these conversations as if they were verbatims. This sudden turn to the past in his chapter entitled "Cases" (70–85) seemed to come out of nowhere and was unfortunate because his extensive use of the mid-nineteenth century book made contemporary church and ministry seem incidental to his pastoral theology program and to his new model of ministry.

Because the case was to represent "all the operations and functions" of the minister and church, it would have been the ideal time for Hiltner to introduce a new form of case, or even multiple types of case, capable of representing many, if not literally all, functions and operations of the church and minister. Instead, he remained with verbatims. At the end of his chapter on healing, Hiltner even warned readers not to assume that his emphasis on conversation between the pastor and individual meant that there was no healing "in sermons, in religious education, in group work, and the like" (1958, 115). He then went on to admit that different facets of church life would have to be examined "for a complete study of pastoral operations from the healing aspect of the shepherding perspective" (115; see also Rodney J. Hunter, 1990, 68).

Because Hiltner did not go beyond the verbatim, the facts of the case in pastoral theology remained the words spoken by the pastor and church member in private conversation as written from memory. Now, however, the dynamic principles to be discovered from the facts were the three aspects of shepherding– healing, sustaining, and guiding. In terms of a method principle, Hiltner discussed the eductive method in guiding. This was the same eductive method of pastoral counseling that he had written about earlier in *Pastoral Counseling* (1949), and he even referred readers to that book (1958, 151–61, 232, endnote 1).

Casebooks: A Genre for Verbatims

Although cases were integral to the modern history of pastoral care education, the case method of teaching actually played only a small role in the teaching of pastoral care and counseling in seminaries once the verbatim was transferred from clinical settings to theological schools. In the case method of teaching, textbooks and lectures would have been replaced entirely by casebooks and case discussion in the classroom. For this to happen, however, teachers would have needed to plan courses based on preexisting cases associated with specific pastoral care topics. Instead, students wrote cases during the semester, foreclosing any such planning. Students read the verbatims of other students and normally were not shown verbatims of teachers or other experienced practitioners. Overall, the use of verbatims for teaching pastoral care in seminaries became more supplementary than primary, as case discussion was combined with lectures and textbooks. It should not be surprising, then, that few pastoral care and counseling casebooks were published in the twentieth century. A casebook without a case method of teaching has no audience.

Dicks's original casebook on hospital ministry, *And Ye Visited Me,* did not inspire imitations. Nor did Hiltner's casebook on pastoral counseling, entitled *The Counselor in Counseling: Case Notes in Pastoral Counseling* (1950). The most extensive pastoral counseling casebook by far was *Casebook in Pastoral Counseling* (1962), edited by Newman Cryer and John Vayhinger. They expressed the hope that more pastoral counseling casebooks would be forthcoming in the years ahead: "We hope that as the quality of pastoral counseling improves new casebooks will appear and become available to each new generation of ministers and ministerial students" (17). Their hope has not been realized, because published verbatims have been used mostly as illustrations in pastoral care and counseling textbooks. Verbatims even began disappearing from the pastoral care and counseling literature toward the end of the twentieth century.

The Decline of Verbatims in the Late Twentieth Century

Everything has its limits, and the verbatim in pastoral care and counseling is no exception. Changes finally began emerging that challenged the facts of the case. Within the church, for example, forms of care not confined to private conversation between the pastor and church member began to be affirmed more strongly. As Gerkin wrote,

> Important as it is, not all care can be expressed through the medium of conversation. Some care can only be given the power of deep connection with communal meanings by way of corporate participation in the symbolic acts of receiving bread and wine, the laying on of hands, and the administration of the water of baptism. Singing together can express care and acknowledge our mutual need for care. Praying together can search for and celebrate the receiving of the care that only God can provide. (1997, 82)

Like Hiltner, however, Gerkin provided no way to study such care.

Another type of change in pastoral care and counseling caused the kinds of principles associated with the verbatim to be challenged. Social, cultural, economic, and political causes of human suffering were explored in pastoral care and counseling during the later years of the twentieth century, though awareness of these issues was not new. Boisen was quite aware of the social dimensions of human suffering and even wrote a book on the sociology of religion. Cabot had helped establish medical social work in the United States, and a case model from social work was used for developing the note-writing format. Cabot and Dicks were not ignorant of social, cultural, economic, or political causes of human suffering but were concerned about hospital patients in situations in which such types of exploration were not in the forefront of concern. The difference at the end of the twentieth century was that many pastoral theologians were no longer willing to set such causes of human suffering aside in favor of an exclusive psychological and spiritual focus on the individual.

Exploration of human suffering from the standpoint of the social sciences did not replace the traditional kinds of principles associated with the verbatim so much as add to them. The psychological dynamics principle, for instance, was not discarded, but neither was it seen as sufficient to account for all human suffering encountered in pastoral care and counseling, such as suffering associated with the oppression of women due to patriarchal traditions. While the care and counseling focus often remained on the individual, couple, or family, the verbatim seemed inadequate for revealing social, cultural, economic, and political factors related to suffering. Because of these and other expansive trends in pastoral care and counseling, such as the influence of postmodern theology, gender concerns, and multicultural issues in pastoral care, verbatims had all but disappeared in the pastoral care and counseling literature by the end of the century. During the 1990s more than in any previous decade, various kinds of narrative vignettes were found where verbatim material would have been found in years past. Often these vignettes were introductions to pastoral psychotherapy clients. With all the change going on in the field, little attention was being paid to the need for new ways to study pastoral care in congregations.

Why New Forms of Case Are Needed for the Congregational Setting

Recently, a new case format for studying pastoral care has been published by Roy Herndon SteinhoffSmith in *The Mutuality of Care* (1999, 198–210). This is a detailed outline and goes far beyond the traditional verbatim. The case format that we will be proposing in the next chapter is different from SteinhoffSmith's, but we do not believe the two should be seen as competitors. In this business of developing case formats in the service of learning pastoral care, we believe that what is good for one is good for all, because the writing and interpreting of cases is a fruitful way of learning pastoral care.

Why, then, are new forms of case needed for studying pastoral care in congregations? The answer really is very simple. It goes back to the reason that Dicks could not transfer the Boisen form of case to the general hospital. It was not a good fit with that setting. Similarly, we are arguing that neither the verbatim nor other forms of case created for use in clinical or other noncongregational settings fits the congregational setting. Certainly, there are points of contact between the congregational and clinical settings. The verbatim could be used, because pastors do have conversations with church members, and sometimes those conversations have some similarity to chaplain and patient conversations. The same can be said with regard to pastoral counseling centers. The problem is that the differences between the settings get shoved aside and ignored as the cases only show what is similar.

In terms of the case method of teaching, this problem can be seen in the facts of the case and the principle contained in those facts. The facts of the case in verbatims and other clinical cases typically leave out much care experience that pastors and church members gain during the normal course of life in the Christian community. The entire issue of worship and care is a case in point. If significant aspects of care in congregations hardly ever get written about in cases, and consequently are rarely if ever reflected in the facts of the case, how can the principles contained in those facts be anything but truncated as far as care in congregations is concerned?

If, as we affirm, writing and interpreting cases is a helpful way of learning pastoral care, cases are needed that enable participants in the church community to write about what they actually are experiencing beyond what is similar to clinical or other settings. This is why, in the next chapter, we are presenting a form of case developed from within the congregational setting.

2

Envisioning the Pastoral Care Case

A new form of case means more than just a different format, a new guideline to follow. It means a new way of thinking about who you are as a case writer and what you are doing when you create a case. It means taking the risk of exposing the pastoral care you practice in the church, along with more of your ministry and even more of your own self, to the view of others than has been the tradition. Taking a risk can be rewarding. Taking the risk of writing and interpreting cases about pastoral care in congregations can yield the reward of learning how to practice pastoral care more effectively, learning more about how it relates to other parts of your ministry, and learning more about yourself.

The name of the new form of case is simply the pastoral care case. It is conceived from within the congregational setting, and it encourages you to tell the story of your pastoral care as you actually are experiencing it. As a pastor, you have a story to tell that is not the same as the ones told by chaplains and pastoral psychotherapists. You know better than anyone else what you are experiencing in pastoral ministry and how this plays out in the realm of care. Using the pastoral care case for learning should enable you to explore this, learn from it, and share it with others so that they can learn more about care in the church. The case method of teaching law was successful because students were enabled to study the very thing they were going to be doing in their practice of law. In the same way, you as a pastor should be able to study the very thing that you and others are doing in congregations in the realm of pastoral care.

The Pastoral Care Case: An Educational Text

One of the most insightful things Cabot and Dicks wrote about case writing was that it involves the creative process of rethinking your pastoral care. Pastoral care case writing facilitates thoughtfulness and reflection about care and evokes moods and feelings and memories associated with care. It involves creating a new text that makes a contribution to learning about the ministry of care as the case is interpreted and its meaning is disclosed and discussed. It even can be seen as spiritual in the sense that it requires the case writer to look within as opposed to just looking back at the past.

The original source for the pastoral care case is the ministry of pastoral care in congregations. Pastoral care in congregations has significant differences from pastoral psychotherapy practiced in pastoral counseling centers and from chaplaincy practiced in medical centers and other institutions. Some differences are obvious, such as lay care, congregational care, and care in preaching and worship as opposed to a pastoral psychotherapy session in a pastoral counseling center, for instance. Other differences, however, are not so obvious. Consider the pastor's care of individual church members. The pastor and church member relationship is not the same as the pastoral psychotherapist and client relationship or the chaplain and patient relationship. First and foremost, the pastor relates to the congregation as a whole, and the pastor's relationships with individual church members develop within the context of this larger relationship. The pastor and congregation relationship is a matrix, or a womb, giving birth to relationships between the pastor and individual church members. It therefore has an important impact on the pastor's care of individuals because, at the very least, it sets up their caring expectations of each other.

A second difference involves the development of the pastor and church member relationship over months and years. The chaplain who enters a hospital room to meet a new patient is encountering a stranger who may return home on the following day and never be seen again. The pastoral psychotherapist who greets a new client is also meeting a stranger who normally will be seen only within the therapy hour and who will not be seen again after termination of treatment. The pastor and church member, however, have a history entering into care, a future extending beyond it, and an ongoing relationship surrounding it, all of which become factors in care.

A third difference involves the multiple ways that the pastor and church member may interact during their relationship. For instance, they may know each other primarily in the context of working together on a committee where the church member may have power as the chairperson. They may interact in a class where the pastor is the teacher and the church member is a student. They may interact in worship, where the pastor is in the role of worship leader and the church member is part of the congregation. They may interact in more informal social roles during church dinners or Sunday school Christmas parties. Personal friendship may grow between them, or they may not like each other particularly. Multiple ways of relating enable the pastor and church member to experience each other in different roles and circumstances. This gives each of them a sense of who they are encountering in care and the kind of behavior to expect. Something may be happening in one or more areas of interaction that facilitates care or, conversely, makes a care encounter awkward for one or both of them, such as conflict in a committee, for instance.

A fourth difference is that pastors sometimes care for church members in the midst of complex circumstances unique to the congregational setting. Specifically, the pastor is also the pastor of other individual church members, couples, families, and groups who may be talked about in care or who may be involved in the care situation. Consider, for instance, a church member who tells the pastor that her husband, also a church member, is having an affair with the choir director, a third church member. In turn, the choir director's husband, yet another church member, also may have talked to the pastor about his suspicion that his wife is having an affair. One or both couples may have children who attend church, as well as other family members who belong to the church, such as parents. Some of them may have friends who are church members and in whom they confide. Moreover, some choir members may be noticing that something is going on and may speak to the pastor or gossip about it. The pastor remains the pastor of each and every individual, couple, family, friend, and group in the church that is talked about or that is involved in the care situation, for they all are part of the congregation.

The pastor's relationship with the congregation as a whole and with individual church members, the multiple ways they relate, and complicating circumstances involving other church members are common aspects of pastoral care in the church community. The pastoral care case writer must be able to write about any and all of these differences, as well as others, if there is to be learning from the original source of pastoral care in congregations.

This raises the question of how best to conceive of the pastoral care case. Certainly, it is an educational text because it is used for learning to practice pastoral care in congregations more effectively. An important educational issue, however, involves finding the best way for case writers to envision the case in order to facilitate the telling of the pastoral care story and to determine the kind of meaning it can be expected to disclose through interpretation.

Each type of text discloses a certain world of meaning. For instance, if you sit down to read a murder mystery, you expect the book to transport you to an imaginary world where a fictional character is killed and other characters solve the horrendous crime. Generally, readers expect a particular type of text to disclose a certain kind of meaning and not anything else. When it comes to the pastoral care case, the same thing is true. It discloses a certain kind of meaning because it is a particular type of text.

The Pastoral Care Case: A Religious Text

One way to envision the pastoral care case as a particular type of text is to view it as a genre. This means simply that the case is a specific sort of text in contrast to other kinds of texts, just as poetry is one sort of text in contrast to the novel. The pastoral care case is a religious genre. It is religious in the sense that its content is about the historic ministry of pastoral care practiced in the church. Consequently, it can be expected that the meaning it discloses through interpretation will be religious, having to do with pastoral care. In the next chapter, the specifics of this meaning will be discussed. Presently, the focus will remain on the case itself seen as a religious genre.

The form of case content plays an important role in determining the kind of meaning that can be disclosed through case interpretation. Because the meaning that the pastoral care case discloses is religious, it will be helpful to see the case as analogous to the biblical forms of discourse. As the coauthor of this book, Donald Capps, has discussed (1984, 21–24), Paul Ricoeur emphasizes that the Bible comprises many different genres, each having its own form, such as narrative, law, prophecy, psalmic hymns, and wisdom. Ricoeur says that the different forms of biblical discourse have something significant in common: Their disclosure of meaning involves revelation in the sense that they all refer to, or name, the same ultimate reality, God. Yet, each of the biblical genres names God differently from all the others. Using musical imagery to communicate this point, he says that the "naming of God...is not simple but multiple. It is not a single tone, but polyphonic" (1979, 220). Each biblical genre names God in a certain tone, so there are as many tones as there are forms of biblical literature. For instance, the exodus story, or narrative, names God through the unfolding of events that bear the "imprint, mark, or trace of God's act" during the course of the story (1980, 77–81). The genre of prophecy, however, reveals God differently, as "the speech of another [God] behind the speech of the prophet" (1980, 75).

Just as the biblical forms of discourse name or reveal God in a variety of tones, so the pastoral care case names or reveals pastoral care in a variety of tones. Like biblical literature, a pastoral care case may contain various forms, all referring to pastoral care. Yet each one refers to care differently, in its own unique tone. Consider, for instance, that one common aspect of pastoral care is prayer and that pastors and church members find themselves praying regularly in pastoral care circumstances. When prayer is represented in a case, it constitutes a certain form of discourse—conversation with God— that differs from all other forms of discourse found in that case. Therefore, a single pastoral care case contains at least two forms of discourse when prayer is included unless there is no discourse other than the prayer, which is relatively rare.

Even when prayer is excluded, the subject matter may assume more than one form. The New Testament gospel helps to show how forms may be related in a case. The gospel as a whole is a genre having a narrative form, containing characters and a plot with a beginning, middle, and end. Yet as the gospel story unfolds, readers encounter a number of additional literary forms that have been woven into the story, such as Jesus' parables, his wisdom sayings, and his proclamations about the coming kingdom. Similarly, the pastoral care case seen as a whole contains a gospel-like narrative in which the case writer becomes a narrator telling the story of pastoral care. In this story, people may be undergoing personal crucifixion and resurrection, suffering and hope. The story may contain gospel-like events, such as the healing of broken relationships and comfort of the bereaved, and there may be Pharisee-like characters and groups in the congregation who are waiting in the wings to pass judgment. As the story progresses, readers may encounter additional forms of discourse woven into the story. One of these may be a proverb-like wisdom saying spoken in a pastoral response. Another may be a parable-like story about seemingly mundane events that discloses new and profound meanings, or proclamation-like sayings as caring people bear witness to God's love.

A certain congregation had a weekly Bible study group led by the associate pastor. This was a relatively small group, and often discussions about the text included examples from members' own lives. One group member was the grandparent of a four-year-old child who had been diagnosed with a brain tumor one month before the latest meeting of the group, so all the group members knew about the diagnosis. So far, the grandparent had not discussed the situation with the group. However, in the most recent meeting, this grandparent could hold back no longer, and the nightmarish story of the previous month began spilling out. The words were directed to the associate pastor as the grandparent's and pastor's eyes locked, but the group as a whole entered into what had become pastoral care.

Woven into the pastoral care narrative unfolding within the Bible study group were two additional forms of discourse, a proverb-like wisdom saying and prayer. The grandparent told a story that began at the doctor's office. The test results were in, and the family gathered in the office to hear what turned out to be devastating news of the tumor. The grandparent told the group about the shock and the tears as the family attempted to cope with this news, and then the grandparent told about the next few weeks of medical treatment, the parents' long hours at the hospital, and lost sleep. At this point, the story took a twist that led to the proverbial form of discourse. Rather than continuing to focus on the recent past, the grandparent shifted to the present and revealed an ongoing inner conflict. The grandchild was in a life-and-death struggle and was suffering greatly. The conflict involved praying for an end to the suffering, which meant death, versus praying for recovered health against great odds. After the grandparent expressed this torturous conflict, there was a short silence. Then the associate pastor said spontaneously, with a gut-level intensity, "Pray for what you really want." This proverb-like statement freed the grandparent to respond in turn, saying, "I want my grandchild to live." This interchange gave birth to the next type of discourse as the grandparent accepted the associate pastor's offer to pray for the child. In this prayer, the pastor expressed the grandparental desire that the child would live, and then went on to pray for the grandparent and for the rest of the family.

This pastoral care story shows that there may be several forms of discourse woven into a larger pastoral care narrative and that they can be seen in analogy to forms of biblical discourse found in the gospel story. Yet this story is hardly on the scale of an entire gospel. Even if more details were given, it still would be like an incident within a chapter of the gospel or like a small chapter at best. The analogy between the pastoral care case and biblical literature focuses on forms of discourse, how they are related, and how they help to determine the meaning that the text can disclose. It does not require that both texts have the same length or complexity. Viewing the analogy in terms of a chapter or part of a chapter within the gospel as a whole is perfectly legitimate where pastoral care is concerned.

Still, in the gospel genre, neither a chapter nor a part of a chapter exists in isolation. Ultimately, each is a part of the gospel as a whole, with a meaning that is related to the larger story, which has implications for understanding the pastoral care story. The pastoral care that happened in the Bible study group did not exist as an isolated event, but, instead, was part of a much larger whole, a pastoral care situation that included many people and that continued over a long period. This care situation involved the senior pastor as well as the associate. They both had been caring for the sick child and the family during the month before the Bible study, and the associate pastor was well aware of the situation before the grandparent spoke about it. In addition to the pastors, individual church members and other groups in the congregation, such as Sunday school classes of the different family members, provided ongoing care. Even the congregation as a whole was involved in the sense of there being a heightened sensitivity to the situation in worship. On the part of the pastors, this was reflected in their preaching, pastoral prayers, and hymn selections.

The pastoral care case as a whole can be a long and involved story and can therefore appear to be like the gospel as a whole. Or it can be fairly short and appear to be like some part of the gospel. Depending on the situation, looking at the various facets of the larger care story and their interconnections can be more significant for learning than focusing on one part exclusively. In terms of case writing, therefore, it is important to allow the length and complexity of the pastoral care case to be determined by the nature of the care situation itself. This is in accord with the view that the pastoral care case is a religious text that reveals, or names, pastoral care in differing tones.

The Self-understanding of the Case Writer

If the pastoral care case is a religious text, who is the case writer? This question has to do with the self-understanding, or authorial identity, of the case writer. The answer is that the pastoral care case writer is a religious author. There are several reasons for this answer, and the first one is quite practical. The pastoral care case writer is a religious author in the sense of being one who creates a religious text about pastoral care in the congregational setting. But additional reasons go beyond this practical one and begin to describe who would write a pastoral care case in the first place.

The second reason for viewing the case writer as a religious author has to do with the church. Paul Tillich wrote that a primary difference between churches and secular institutions involves the church's conscious representation of its "Spiritual" foundation through "manifest religious self-expression" (1963, 153). In order to be congruent with the church, the pastoral care case writer participates in this "manifest religious self-expression" by developing the self-understanding of a religious author who writes about the ministry of pastoral care.

The third reason is that the self-understanding of the case writer should be congruent with that writer's larger identity as a pastor or church member. For pastors, this means that the case writer understands case writing to be an integral part of what a pastor does for the preparation, practice, and study of ministry in the church and, more specifically, for growth in the ministry of pastoral care without stepping outside one's evolving pastoral identity. For church members, this means something similar. Being a religious author should be congruent with one's larger identity as a believer who participates in the community of faith.

The fourth reason takes into account what pastoral care is like in the congregational setting. For example, pastoral care often occurs intermingled with other facets of congregational life and ministry. Its scope may range from a focus on individuals to one on families, groups, and the congregation as a whole, and it may involve one or more areas of suffering out of countless possibilities. Consequently, the case writer's self-understanding is that of one who is concerned with the entire extent of pastoral care as it is manifest in congregations.

Like any author, the case writer naturally is concerned with the concrete issue of how to write a case. This concern leads to three issues that case writers must address. The first is the source of the case content. The second is its style, and the third is the format in which it is to be written.

The Source of Case Content

Pastoral care in which the case writer participates is the source that the case writer uses for creating the subject matter comprising the pastoral care case, and the author must figure out how to draw on this source to facilitate writing. With this in mind, it is helpful to contrast pastoral care case writing with verbatim writing, since the source of both involves pastoral care in which the writer participates.

The source of a verbatim is a single pastoral care conversation in which the verbatim writer participates. The way that the verbatim writer draws on this source is by using memory to reproduce the conversation in writing, which becomes the content of the verbatim. This puts a heavy burden on the verbatim writer's memory, but it is commonly observed that memory improves with verbatim writing experience. Given that perfect memory is an unreachable ideal, however, every verbatim is flawed to some unknowable degree. Nevertheless, such flawed content traditionally has been deemed acceptable for education because writing and analyzing a verbatim have been seen as important for learning regardless of the imperfect content.

The verbatim writing process can be seen from the standpoint of hermeneutical theory having to do with spoken discourse, or speaking and listening. Ricoeur (1976) says that human beings experience spoken discourse in two interrelated ways. Seen from the standpoint of speaking, the words being spoken are an event that happens, and they are gone as soon as the sound of their being spoken ceases. Discourse being spoken is "realized temporally and in a present moment" (11). However, from the standpoint of listening to what is being spoken, the words are understood as meaning rather than simply as an event. "If all discourse is actualized as an event, all discourse is understood as meaning" (12). The meaning comes from the words and sentences themselves that are being spoken and includes the message being communicated. It is the "intertwining of noun and verb...insofar as it endures" (12). Spoken discourse understood as meaning is not transient, but remains, or is "retained as the *same* meaning" (12). Imagine the impossibility of communication if the meaning of spoken discourse disappeared as do the sounds of words after they are spoken.

In this semantic light, verbatim writers have tended to err on the side of viewing spoken discourse as an event being actualized. Consequently, when pastoral care conversation becomes the source of verbatim writing, it tends to be seen solely as a temporal event to be remembered and reproduced in writing. Consideration of meaning is reserved for interpretation of the verbatim. Yet because the pastoral care discourse that the verbatim writers actually remember is understood as meaning, the written discourse of the verbatim already contains implicit interpretation preceding the analysis. This is because understanding discourse as meaning happens through an interpretive process.

This brings us to pastoral care case writing, which differs from verbatim writing in two primary ways. The first difference involves the source. The source of verbatim writing, a single care conversation, by no means exhausts pastoral care in the congregational setting. Care in congregations may be ongoing; it may include a variety of circumstances; and it may involve different people or groups. Even when it involves private conversation between the pastor and church member, that conversation may be part of a larger care situation that is essential for understanding the conversation. Therefore, the source drawn upon for pastoral care case writing is not confined to single conversations between the pastor and church member, though it does not exclude them. Instead, the source includes the full extent of pastoral care as it occurs in congregations.

For instance, immediately following worship one Sunday, the pastor of a small church in a large city received word that a former member had just died. The deceased was an elderly woman who had moved to a distant suburb one year ago to live with family and had transferred her membership to their church at that time. After moving, she still maintained contact with some longtime friends in her old church, and it was this group of friends that the pastor comforted after worship that day. The care happened through a series of conversations as the pastor approached the friends of this woman individually during the coffee hour following worship to inform them of her death. Any one of these conversations could provide material for a verbatim, but a verbatim would not give the pastor the means of writing about an essential part of what was experienced that Sunday morning or about the rest of the care situation as it unfolded. The series of conversations, rather than any one of them individually, enabled the pastor to realize gradually that the woman had significance for her friends as a group beyond their various personal relationships with her. It turned out that eight years ago, five years before the pastor came to the congregation, these friends and the deceased woman had transferred their memberships to the church after the one they had belonged to for many years closed. The woman became a kind of matriarchal figure, helping the group maintain a sense of cohesiveness as they gradually adjusted to their new church and as they grieved the loss of their defunct congregation. During the days before the woman's funeral, the pastor also learned that this group had always felt like "second-class citizens" in their new congregation. On reflection, the pastor realized that indeed there was something to this. There did seem to be at least two tiers of membership, and this group was in the lower rank. Then came the funeral, in which the pastor was asked to represent the woman's former church by saying a few words. Having learned some of this history, the pastor was able to speak about the woman in a way that was meaningful to the group of friends, and this was a significant part of the pastor's care for them, along with private conversation.

In this situation, pastoral care began when the pastor received news of the woman's death. It continued through several days and included conversations with different people, and the funeral itself. It required that the schedule of the pastor be revised and a meeting postponed, and the pastor was asked to drive some of the friends to the funeral home for the funeral. Although any part of the situation could be singled out for analysis, the pastor did not experience it as a series of isolated events but instead as a meaningful care situation that was unfolding and that culminated with the funeral. If the pastor were to write a pastoral care case about this care situation, the situation as a whole would be the source. The case could include quotes from conversation, but it also could include such things as a narrative of the situation as a whole, discussion of the congregation as it relates to the group of friends, and what the pastor said in the funeral.

The second contrast between pastoral care case writing and verbatim writing involves how the case writer draws on the source for writing. It is helpful to think of drawing on this source through self-reflection rather than through memory in which the writer strains to remember each and every word exactly as it was spoken. In self-reflection, the case writer focuses inward and may spend time quietly listening for what wants to emerge from within about the care. Such reflection includes memory, but as part of self-reflection it is a more wide-ranging kind of remembering that is typical of human beings as they recall events, circumstances, and conversations. It is the kind of remembering that enables the case writer to narrate the story of pastoral care.

Within the context of self-reflection, pastoral care conversation is remembered as meaning because, like all speaking, it is understood as meaning. When one person is listening to another person speak, the words being spoken are not comprehended simply in terms of their being a temporal event that happens and then is over. Rather, what is spoken is understood in terms of what the words and sentences mean and in terms of the message being communicated. This meaning remains available to everyone in the conversation in the sense that they can talk further about it. They can clarify it, interpret it, explore it, correct it, challenge it, repeat it, or paraphrase it. In pastoral care case writing, some of this meaning that remains can be remembered, and some may be forgotten. Some may be repeated, and some may be summarized. Ultimately, what is important for case writing is not merely remembering more conversation but rather growing in the ability to engage in self-reflection for drawing on the source of case writing. In the final chapter, we will develop the related theme of introspection in case writing.

Out of this self-reflection, the case writer creates new written discourse that becomes the content of the pastoral care case. This content is not fiction made up out of thin air, as if the only source were the case writer's imagination. Nor is it data in the scientific sense. Rather, it is a religious text about the case writer's pastoral care.

Style and Pastoral Care Case Writing

Style can be very revealing. There is nowhere to hide when it comes to style because it is about individuality, or uniqueness. Each pastoral care case has style, or a unique configuration of written discourse distinguishing it from all other cases. As an example, consider two of the synoptic gospels, Mark and Matthew, and imagine for a moment that they are pastoral care cases. Mark begins his case by quoting Isaiah, and then he moves directly to John's baptizing people in the Jordan. In Mark's very first chapter, Jesus is introduced as one who is baptized by John and who travels to the wilderness immediately following the baptism: "And the Spirit immediately drove him out into the wilderness. He was in the wilderness forty days, tempted by Satan; and he was with the wild beasts; and the angels waited on him" (vv. 12–13).

At first glance, Mark appears to be presenting the bare bones of a story that could be passed over quickly in the context of reading the entire chapter. A closer look shows that this passage contains description that raises many questions but provides no answers. There is no elaboration or explanation of what it means to be driven somewhere by the Spirit, or to be tempted by Satan, or to be waited on by angels. More importantly, the reader is told neither the nature of the temptation nor whether Jesus succumbed or resisted.

Matthew, writing within the same gospel genre, tells the same temptation story quite differently. He begins his case with a genealogy of Jesus and follows this with the story of Jesus' birth. Not until the third chapter does he introduce John the Baptist, who baptizes Jesus. Then, like Mark, Matthew tells about the temptation of Jesus in the wilderness:

> Then Jesus was led up by the Spirit into the wilderness to be tempted by the devil. He fasted forty days and forty nights, and afterwards he was famished. The tempter came and said to him, "If you are the Son of God, command these stones to become loaves of bread." But he answered, "It is written, 'One does not live by bread alone, but by every word that comes from the mouth of God.'" Then the devil took him to the holy city and placed him on the pinnacle of the temple, saying to him, "If you are the Son of God, throw yourself down; for it is written, 'He will command his angels concerning you,' and 'On their hands they will bear you up, so that you will not dash your foot against a stone.'" Jesus said to him, "Again it is written, 'Do not put the Lord your God to the test.'" Again, the devil took him to a very high mountain and showed him all the kingdoms of the world and their splendor; and he said to him, "All these I will give you, if you will fall down and worship me." Jesus said to him, "Away with you, Satan! for it is written, 'Worship the Lord your God, and serve only him.'" Then the devil left him, and suddenly angels came and waited on him. (4:1–11)

Matthew develops the story in much more detail than Mark through additional description and by adding dialogue. Now, Jesus not only is driven into the wilderness by the Spirit, he is driven there for the purpose of being tempted by the devil. In addition to being there for forty days, he is fasting during this time. Ultimately, the reader finds out about the temptation and its outcome through its presentation as a discussion between Jesus and the devil, complete with quotes.

The contrast between the styles disclosed in Mark and Matthew is great. Each contains a unique configuration of discourse that cannot be mistaken for the other. One gives minimal description while the other provides details and extensive discussion. So it is with the pastoral care case. Each case reflects a certain style, or individuality, distinguishing it from other cases. One case may resemble Mark, leaving the reader with many questions, while another may be more like Matthew.

Style is associated with the case writer because writing is what produces that unique configuration of case discourse. During the course of writing a case, the writer makes decisions that help determine the style. A decision as simple and seemingly mundane as whether to place a period or exclamation point at the end of a sentence can contribute to style, and it certainly affects the meaning disclosed. In modern translations, Matthew provides an illustration of the dramatic difference punctuation can make by injecting an exclamation point into the middle of a sentence spoken by Jesus at the end of the temptation story. In verse 4:10, Jesus says, "Away with you, Satan! for it is written." The inclusion of this exclamation point helps disclose the force in this statement. Jesus is speaking with the force of a command, or at least an exasperated request. He is very animated, full of feeling as he speaks. Omission of the exclamation point would reveal a very different image of Jesus, one in which he is not as emotionally involved when he speaks. The same would be true of any character in a case.

Another type of decision affecting style involves the way in which sentences and paragraphs are constructed. Everything from the title to the introduction to descriptions to quotes can be written in a variety of ways. A mechanical and seemingly factual style can be used to represent a smile, for instance. The case writer may write, "the church member smiled," but this may not be as factual as believed because human beings exhibit a broad range of smiles, from very slight to a big grin. The smile may be congruent with the words being spoken, or it may be a thinly veiled mask hiding pain. Thus, in some instances, a more creative style is called for, even to the point of using metaphor. For example, instead of just writing, "the church member smiled," the writer may use "Mona Lisa smile," or "sly smile," or "a grin from ear to ear." Decisions about how to describe something that happened in pastoral care may not seem huge in themselves, but they do affect the style.

A third type of decision affecting style involves editing the content of the case in the sense of deciding what to include, what to omit, and what to summarize when there is a large amount of material to be discussed. For example, a particular instance of pastoral care may have involved a lengthy conversation that could fill up seven or eight pages if written out in its entirety, while the case writer may want to confine this material to two or three pages of conversation. Such a circumstance requires the case writer to make editing decisions, and these decisions contribute to the uniqueness of each case.

The Pastoral Care Case Format

A format is a set of rules, or instructions, used to guide writing so that what is written will be arranged in a particular way. For instance, when a professor tells a class that a term paper must be no longer than twenty-five pages, the professor is giving an instruction that is part of the format governing the length of the paper. Because the case writer is telling the story of pastoral care, the pastoral care case format is designed to help case writers do just that, tell the story in writing.

The Title

The initial part of the pastoral care case is the title. This is an appropriate place to begin case writing because the title is the first point of communication with readers. What, then, should the title communicate? Much as a good sermon title in the worship bulletin lets church members know something about the upcoming sermon, so the pastoral care case title should tell readers about the main theme of the case, such as "Pastoral Care with an Engaged Couple" or "Mrs. Jones's Bereavement." Because writing a title first requires that the case writer identify the main theme, creating the title provides a good entry point into the self-reflection needed for drawing on the source, or the pastoral care about which the case is being written. Thus, the initial part of self-reflection may be to focus on the question of what the pastoral care is about overall. Within the context of this question posed to oneself, the first part of remembering the pastoral care may be to survey it as a whole and move from its beginning to its middle to its end. Perhaps along the way, some part of it will stand out and provide the case writer with the information needed to name the theme.

When the main theme is immediately evident to the case writer, it is unnecessary to focus on the title in this way. Yet the main theme of pastoral care is not always clear, especially if there are complicating circumstances and more than one or two people involved. At any rate, the title is as good as any other part of the case for beginning self-reflection and using the source for writing the case.

The Introduction

The introduction has two parts. In the first part, introduce yourself as the author of the case. Tell a little about yourself. Include such things as your age, gender, race, ethnicity, and marital status. Next, discuss your involvement with the congregation from which the case comes. Are you a pastor, an associate pastor, a seminary student in field education, a church member? How long have you been in this position? What is your denomination? Finally, is there anything in particular that would be important or helpful for readers to know about you regarding the case? What bubbles to the surface in your reflection?

Introducing yourself as the case author may seem to be an obvious thing to do because the case is about your pastoral care and you hope to learn from it. There is another reason to do so, however. In addition to being the author, you play two interrelated roles in the case. You are the narrator who is telling the story of pastoral care, and simultaneously you are one of the characters participating in that care. You are author, narrator, and character. By writing yourself into the story in these ways, you are taking the risk of inviting case readers into your life, and you do not have control over what they may learn about you through their interpretations. Consequently, there is a moral dimension to this educational process in the sense that you are opening yourself to the critique of case readers and in the sense that they have a responsibility not to abuse you or manipulate you after you have opened yourself to critique. This moral dimension has educational value. On the one hand, you may recognize that the vulnerability, fear, and hope that come with the territory of openness to critique perhaps has some similarity to the vulnerability, fear, and hope that church members may have when they take the risk of opening themselves to your care. On the other hand, the way case readers treat you in your state of openness may reveal something about their caring abilities. This is one way that your case writing can help others learn as well as help you.

In the second part of the introduction, pick up where you left off with the title by providing an overview of what you perceive to be the main theme of the case. Here is a brief example from one pastor: "I was sitting at my desk last Thursday afternoon when I received a phone call. It was Ruth asking if she and her fiancé, Mark, could stop by the office to talk to me about their wedding. We made an appointment for 4:00 p.m. the next afternoon, and during our discussion, the main theme of the conversation was the couple's concern about the participation of Mark's family in the wedding." At this point, the reader naturally would assume that the case is about this conversation in the pastor's office, focusing on the couple's concern. This is not much information, however, and questions arise. Perhaps it is a one-time pastoral counseling encounter, and not much more needs to be said about it. Or perhaps it is part of a larger situation, and the case writer needs to set this encounter within a broader context. There could have been a series of premarital counseling sessions, and the meaning of this one will not be made clear without the larger story. Perhaps Mark's family has been discussed before, and the pastor is familiar with the issue. Yet we do not know whether Ruth or Mark or their families are church members or whether the pastor knows them. Moreover, this may be part of an ongoing pastoral care situation that may include the wedding itself. The conversation may be only a small part of the overall situation. Or perhaps the real issue is the pastor's anxiety over dealing with Mark's family. The point is that different amounts of detail can be given in the introduction, and different directions can be taken. It is up to the case writer to make a judgment about detail and direction before moving on to the next section of the case.

This is not a trivial issue, because one part of learning pastoral care in the congregational setting is learning to judge the complexity of care and the appropriate degree of your involvement in it. Pastors practice many other facets of ministry along with care and need to make such judgments. Some care situations appropriately need only a single encounter. Other care situations are chronic and can eat up too much of your time, energy, and soul if appropriate boundaries for spending time with the situation are not established. One of the interesting things about pastoral ministry is that it includes so much diversity, including care. As a case writer, you have a story to tell that may take unusual turns, that may be fairly simple and straightforward, or that may be unduly complex and confusing. Only you can tell the story of pastoral care as you experience it, and therefore only you know what needs to be included in the introduction or in any other part of the case.

The Congregational Setting

In this part of the story, introduce the congregation, discussing it in relation to the main theme of the pastoral care that you wrote about in the previous section. You may never have written about a congregation before, and it may seem strange to think in terms of its various characteristics, much less in terms of how it is related to pastoral care. Basically, all you need to do is take a step back, look at your congregation as a whole, and imagine that you are telling the reader about it.

Begin by sharing with readers the name of your congregation and its denomination. If there is a pastoral staff, give a little information about them. Tell about various characteristics of the congregation, including such things as its size and age, features of the membership, its socioeconomic status, and its racial and ethnic makeup. It may be a historic downtown church that draws from all over the city (and surrounding states), or it may be an older, declining congregation tucked away in a neighborhood. It may be wealthy or poor. It may have a proud tradition of local mission or be known for its music. It may be on the path to renewal or on the road toward death. It may be filled to the brim with toddlers and parents because it is in just the right suburban location, or conversely, it may have a majority of seniors.

Every congregation exists within a larger community, so next tell about the community in which your church resides. It may be urban or suburban. It may be a rural area or a small town. It may be a section of the city that is changing dramatically for better or for worse. It may be a highway out in the county in an area of declining population. It may be a culturally, racially, and ethnically diverse community that has an international flavor. It may be quite wealthy. It may be blue-collar. It may be in transition, or it may be very stable.

Communities in which churches reside participate in society with its political and economic processes, and they participate in culture with its values. So these things also can be part of the discussion as needed.

Tell about the theological orientation of the congregation. As you have experienced it, how would you characterize the theology of the congregation? Is there theological diversity, or does everyone seem to think alike theologically? How does the theological orientation of the congregation fit with your personal theological understanding? Is it a perfect fit, or do you struggle with it? Why?

Discuss the way in which the congregation, as a whole or any relevant aspect of it, is related to the main theme of the pastoral care that you discussed in the previous section. It may be a piece of congregational history, some conflict, a group or committee in the congregation that is involved directly in the pastoral care situation. Is the local community a factor in some way? Is a theological theme related to the pastoral care? For example, in the pastor's care of Ruth and Mark mentioned above, the church's theological understanding of marriage turned out to be an important factor. Ruth was a member of the church, which was Protestant. Mark came from a Roman Catholic family, and his parents were upset that he was considering joining Ruth's church. In addition, they did not like the differences in wedding ceremonies. Regardless of the pastor's personal opinion about this matter, the church's explicit theological understanding of marriage and policies related to marriage were real factors in this situation, and in the contemporary world, the understanding of marriage is no small matter.

The Characters

The story of pastoral care includes a discussion of those who are participating in the pastoral care. In addition to the case writer, there is at least one other character to be discussed. Begin by identifying this person and giving some basic information. Is the person male or female; Caucasian, African American, Hispanic, or Asian; young, middle-aged, or elderly; single, married, or divorced; a parent or grandparent? How is the person related to the congregation? What do you know about the family of the person?

More than one individual may be involved in the pastoral care. If so, discuss each of them along with any couples, families, or groups that may be involved.

If the pastoral care is about caring for a troubled congregation, the congregation as a whole may be the main character. In this instance, because you already introduced the congregation in the previous section, you must judge what part of the discussion of the congregation goes in the previous section and what part goes in this section. For example, in the previous section the emphasis can be on the congregation as a whole, and in this section the emphasis can be on the main people, groups, and aspects of local community that are associated with your care of the troubled congregation.

You, the case writer, also are a character. Although you have been discussed in the introduction, now you become part of the discussion again by telling about the history of your relationship with each of the other characters. When did you first meet? How do you usually relate to each other? Have you cared for the person, couple, family, group, or troubled congregation before? Are you relative strangers, or have you become friends? How did your relationship affect the pastoral care, and how did the pastoral care affect your relationship?

Let's pick up again with Ruth and Mark. Ruth is a twenty-nine-year-old Caucasian female. She has been divorced for three years and has custody of her two small children, Jane and Peter. Once again, the case writer has many possibilities in terms of what to include and omit and in terms of how the story is told. Perhaps she is a lifelong member of the congregation, and her divorce had a strong impact on a number of church members. Or perhaps she has been a church member for only six months and hardly knows anyone in the church. Regarding the divorce, it may or may not be important for the pastor to go into detail. Part of this history may involve Ruth's ex-husband. Is her ex-husband a church member, or did he leave the congregation at the time of the divorce? Does he have family that belongs to the church? Did the couple have mutual friends in the church? How was the congregation affected by the divorce, especially family and friends who remain in the congregation?

The history of the pastor's relationship with Ruth may vary widely, also. Perhaps the pastor has known Ruth for many years. Or perhaps the pastor was new at the church when the divorce happened, and the pastor initially got to know her by caring for her and her children during that difficult time and in its aftermath. Perhaps the pastor and Ruth gradually expanded their relationship through various areas of church involvement. Or perhaps Ruth remained on the edge of the congregation, and the pastor hardly ever saw her.

Discussion of Ruth's family may vary in significance and length. It may be that the pastor knows little or nothing about her family of origin because they are not church members. What little is known may come from what was learned during the time of the divorce. Another possibility, however, is that her parents are movers and shakers in the congregation, so the pastor has frequent encounters with them and has come to know their concerns about Ruth and their grandchildren. Perhaps the pastor's care over time has begun to span three generations. As a result, the pastor's care of Ruth may include insightful perception of her in relation to her parents, her children, and the congregation but also is colored by these multiple relationships.

The other main character is Mark, a Caucasian male who looks like he is in his early thirties. Ruth met Mark one year following her divorce and eventually invited him to church. The pastor's primary contact with him has been on those Sunday mornings when he accompanies Ruth to church. Now their relationship is expanding, however. When Mark and Ruth became engaged and asked the pastor to marry them, the pastor began learning more about Mark through conversation with the couple. Mark has been divorced for five years and obtained custody of his only child, Margaret, through a prolonged court battle. Now he wants to join Ruth's congregation and to have his daughter join, which is a significant part of what is causing tension in his family of origin. It is only through such conversation with Mark that the pastor will learn anything about Mark's family, and the pastor may be in the awkward position of meeting them for the first time at the wedding rehearsal.

The final character is Mark and Ruth as a couple and the history of the pastor's relationship with the couple. For instance, the pastor may be just finding out about one troubling aspect of their relationship. As single parents, Ruth and Mark know the seemingly never-ending trials and tribulations of dealing with ex-spouses in relation to the children. Now that they are getting married, those trials and tribulations already are taking on a whole new dimension. The pastor may have learned about this through discussion with the couple or may just have secondhand knowledge based on comments by a parent or friend, which should be taken with a grain of salt. The couple may or may not invite the pastor into conversation about this issue.

Telling What Happened

In the final section of the case, tell what happened during the pastoral care. Several directions can be taken in this section. In one direction, the case writer can tell about a single pastoral care encounter. The conversation that Mark and Ruth had with the pastor in the church office is an example. In this instance, the case writer can tell about the conversation using a combination of description and quotes in a narrative arrangement:

> I listened intently as Mark began talking about his mother's opposition to the marriage. Mark said, "Two nights ago, we got into a big fight about Ruth…"

> By the time Mark finished telling about the fight, Ruth was visibly shaken. She looked at Mark and said, "I can't believe your mother would say that!" Mark looked down at the floor.

Another possibility is to tell about a series of pastoral care encounters. If, for example, Mark and Ruth had spoken to the pastor in the office three times over a four-week period, the pastor as case writer could discuss all the encounters rather than singling out one of them. In this instance, there would be less detail given about one encounter and more attention given to developments taking place over the course of the three encounters. Or there could be events going on between the meetings that should be discussed. Perhaps the pastor's own marital situation calls for reflection because it is influencing the meetings.

A third possibility is to tell about a pastoral care situation. If it is unfolding over weeks and months, it may defy easy characterization as an encounter, as a series of encounters, or as a conversation. It may include all these things and much more, such as different kinds of congregational circumstances, a variety of care participants, and worship. For example, consider another engaged couple, Joan and Rick. Plans were on track, and the wedding was three months away. Then tragedy struck. Joan's mother died suddenly and unexpectedly. There was a funeral at the church where the wedding was to take place. There was discussion about whether or not to postpone the wedding. Then there was the wedding, which included a strange mixture of joy and sorrow. As one member of the wedding party commented, "This is the only wedding I've been to where I got choked up, but not because the couple was getting married." In telling about this pastoral care situation, the pastor may include some material from the funeral, some discussion of care conversation, some description of circumstances, and some material from the wedding. The case writer, the narrator, may include whatever is needed in order to tell the story of pastoral care in the congregational setting.

Conclusion

Case writers are free to tell the story of pastoral care complete with all the circumstances and interconnections with other aspects of ministry and church life that come with the territory of pastoral care in congregations. This story deserves telling and studying not only because effective pastoral care can make a difference in human lives but also because pastoral care is a historic ministry of the church that teaches us about bearing one another's burdens in the context of community.

3

Meaning and the Pastoral Care Case

In the first chapter, the procedure for interpreting cases was introduced because learning from cases requires knowing how to interpret them. In the second chapter, the pastoral care case was introduced because learning about pastoral care in congregations requires a case about that subject. Now, in this chapter, the kind of meaning that the pastoral care case discloses through interpretation is introduced because improving the practice of pastoral care requires encountering that meaning.

Case Meaning and Interpretation

The meaning associated with a pastoral care case goes hand-in-hand with the interpretive process. Without interpretation, the case will not disclose its meaning. Interpretation provides a way of proceeding that involves identifying the facts of the case and discerning the principle contained in them, and it also provides pastoral care principles for evaluating the facts of the case so that the principle as it is contained in those facts can be revealed.

Seen from the standpoint of the case method of teaching, one primary function of the interdisciplinary dialogue in pastoral theology is to provide pastoral care principles for evaluating the facts of the case in pastoral care education. This is the dialogue that brings theology and the social sciences into conversation. The inter-disciplinary models, or care principles, resulting from this dialogue have been applied in pastoral counseling centers, in chaplaincy, and in congregational settings over the years. Yet differences between the settings rarely, if ever, have been taken into account, as if the interdisciplinary models could be used in any setting without regard for differences between them. To some extent this is understandable, given the prevalence of the verbatim, whose facts of the case consist of private conversation. The verbatim portrays pastors of churches, pastoral psychotherapists, and chaplains as practicing pastoral care in exactly the same way. Yet even when considering the congregational setting by itself, portraying pastoral care in exactly the same way in all cases is a distortion.

Because principles of care are so important for understanding the meaning that the pastoral care case discloses, it will be helpful to identify some differences between the congregational setting and clinical settings, including the use of theology, psychology, and other social sciences within them. Consider some ways that the specialized ministry of pastoral psychotherapy, conducted in the pastoral counseling center setting, differs from pastoral care and counseling in the congregational setting.

First, pastoral psychotherapists, for sound therapeutic reasons, refrain from associating with clients outside the therapy hour. Pastoral psychotherapists and their clients do not play tennis or go to the movies together. Clients are not invited to the pastoral psychotherapist's home to meet family or friends. Normally, the only times they ever have contact with each other is within the pastoral psychotherapy sessions. The opposite situation prevails in pastoral ministry, however. Compared to the pastoral psychotherapist, the pastor's life is an open book, even to church members who seek the pastor for counseling. The church member turned counselee may very well have played tennis with the pastor, may have been in the pastor's home the day before the pastoral counseling session, or may have been visited in the hospital by the pastor. This requires the pastor to be more varied in approach than the pastoral psychotherapist.

A second difference involves theology in the two settings. The pastoral psychotherapist develops a theological perspective in the context of practicing pastoral psychotherapy with the use of psychotherapeutic method. This theological perspective usually remains private, within the understanding of the pastoral psychotherapist, rather than being discussed with the client explicitly.

The pastor of a congregation must develop a theological perspective that is not so heavily concentrated on pastoral care and counseling, pastoral psychotherapy, or the dialogue between theology and psychology. Instead, it encompasses the full spectrum of theological issues present in the church. In particular, the pastor's theological perspective develops in relation to the internal life of the congregation, its mission in the local community and in the world, and the whole of ministry. The pastor is a public figure whose theological perspective is available for all to see week after week in worship leadership and in such activities as Bible studies.

These theological differences influence practice. For instance, Mrs. Jones goes to a pastoral counseling center and enters psychotherapy. She may or may not belong to a church or be religious. She most likely will never know the denomination of the pastoral psychotherapist. She probably will never know the theological standpoint from which the pastoral psychotherapist sees her or the psychotherapy. As one pastoral psychotherapist says: "I admit to quite a difference between the conversations I had as a pastor with parishioners and those I have as a pastoral counselor, and to some extent that is as it should be. One difference is my hesitance in claiming and using ritual authority in a more specialized, clinical setting" (Nancy J. Gorsuch, 1999, 38). She elaborates by explaining why she does not pray with some clients: "They do not necessarily acknowledge my pastoral authority, and we do not often share a language of faith so fully as when I functioned as a pastor. We do not share experiences of corporate worship or fellowship and mission in the life of a community of faith, and so the language of faith seems almost intrusive, interrupting the conversation rather than facilitating it" (38–39). On the other hand, another woman, Mrs. Wallace, goes to see her pastor for a pastoral counseling session in the pastor's office. She participates in the life of the church and does share experiences of worship, fellowship, and mission with the pastor and other church members, and as a result she has a reasonably good idea of the pastor's theological orientation. For the pastor and for Mrs. Wallace, the theology is that of the church and is therefore something they hold in common, not to say, of course, that there can be no theological variance or even conflict between them.

There also are differences in the psychological perspectives developed in the two settings. In the pastoral counseling center, the psychological perspective is developed within the context of pastoral psychotherapy practice and is related intimately to psychotherapeutic method as it plays out in the sessions. For example, one typical part of the psychological perspective is a model of human development associated with the particular psychotherapeutic method being used. In the congregational setting, however, there is no way to prevent the separation of a psychological understanding of human beings from psychotherapeutic practice, because the pastor's daily ministry involves explicit religious leadership in the church as opposed to the daily practice of pastoral psychotherapy. Pastors have the opportunity to gain extensive psychological knowledge of church members during the course of their life together in the Christian community. Consequently, when a pastor practices pastoral care or counseling in the congregation, the psychological perspective cannot be dissociated from its larger context as if the pastor had developed the psychological perspective solely within the practice of pastoral counseling.

A similar point can be made about other social sciences. In pastoral theology, different social or behavioral sciences, such as sociology, cultural anthropology, economics, and political science, are used to identify causes of human suffering in addition to psychological causes. "The social sciences represent a rich primary source for the development and continued formation of pastoral care and counseling. This is especially true as increasing amounts of social science research have come to focus upon the social conditions which detrimentally affect personal adjustment and well-being" (Balswick, 1990, 1193). When additional social science perspectives are used in the specialized pastoral counseling center context with its psychotherapeutic method, they take their place alongside the psychological perspective. In the congregational setting, however, social science perspectives in addition to psychology are not developed within pastoral care or pastoral counseling primarily, but instead have to do with pastoral ministry as a whole and the life of the church in the local community and larger world. In preaching, teaching, evangelism, and mission, pastors have to deal with society, culture, gender, national debates over moral issues, and so on. And just as they have the opportunity to gain psychological knowledge of church members, they also have the opportunity to see the impact on church members and on the congregation as a whole of the local community; family dynamics; social, economic, and political systems; cultural values; and multicultural situations. This knowledge may help pastors in pastoral care or pastoral counseling situations, but there simply is not the same need to squeeze every perspective into dual pastoral theology categories of theology and social science as there is when the focus is on pastoral psychotherapy.

Given the differences between settings in which pastoral care is practiced, neither the facts of the case nor interpretive perspectives can be taken for granted. This makes it especially important to name the facts of the case in the pastoral care case.

Identifying the Facts of the Pastoral Care Case

In the pastoral care case, the facts of the case include the full scope of pastoral care as it occurs in congregations. The scope of care in congregations is its range, or the distance over which it extends. As we saw in chapter two, the pastoral care case format allows case authors to write about what they are experiencing in pastoral care, which provides for a wide range of possible care scenarios. Consequently, the scope of care may vary from case to case, so that pastoral care cases may have real differences from one another as opposed to the sameness of verbatims. In light of these possible differences, it is helpful to characterize the scope of pastoral care in terms of what can be called its distinguishing features, which means that care has certain discernible characteristics, traits, or properties. Together, the distinguishing features of pastoral care in the congregational setting make up the scope of care. One case may emphasize some distinguishing features and be quite different from another case because of the particular configuration of features contained in that case. In pastoral care case interpretation, the facts of the case to be identified are the distinguishing features of pastoral care in congregations.

The First Distinguishing Feature

The first distinguishing feature of pastoral care in the congregational setting involves identifying the pastoral care situation, the main problem being addressed in the case. In the early 1930s, when Russell Dicks began writing down his conversations with individual hospital patients, he was writing about individuals who were physically ill. In the congregational setting, the possible kinds of problems are far more expansive. The types of problems are as varied as those who participate in pastoral care. They may involve such things as mental and physical illness, death, funerals, bereavement, marital and family problems, job loss, divorce, child custody issues, addiction, various kinds of violence and abuse, conflict between church members, poverty, oppression, personal crises, and emergencies. Such problems as these have been listed in pastoral care literature for many years. Yet in pastoral care education there has been no determination of which problems are most consistently encountered in the church and need the most attention. Moreover, personal, social, and political dimensions of emotionally explosive issues, such as abortion, have become so interwoven in today's world that it is difficult to identify, much less limit, the range of care regarding identifying both the types of problems and the methods of solving them. A single pastoral care case obviously does not contain all the possible difficulties encountered in pastoral care. It should be possible to name the problem or problems going on in the case.

The Second Distinguishing Feature

The second distinguishing feature involves identifying the characters in the case. These may be individuals, couples, families, groups, the congregation, or the community. In this sense, scope may range from the individual to the congregation and community, with every possible grouping of characters in between. More is involved in this identification, however.

In the congregational setting, the laity who make up the church, as well as the ordained clergy, practice pastoral care. Church members are not always on the receiving end of care, which has been readily acknowledged in pastoral care literature during the 1990s. They practice it with one another and with others in the local community in the context of local mission. To care for others is an inherent part of Christian life that cannot be confined to an official aspect of professional ministry. It may occur within small groups, Sunday school classes, and friendships. Pastoral care may happen as church members respond to emergencies. There may be groups in larger congregations who are organized specifically for practicing care and who receive special care training. Any pastor who has walked into a hospital room or home to visit a church member in crisis only to find other church members already there knows that the amount of pastoral care in the congregation is much greater than that provided by the ordained clergy alone. The occasions for care in the congregation transcend what is possible during the traditional clergy call in the community and conversation in the office. Caring activities, such as bearing one another's burdens, comforting the bereaved, responding to crises, feeding the hungry, and making contact with those confined to their homes or to institutions, may happen during the course of church life even without the minister's knowledge. Imagine the absurdity of the ordained minister's having to know when each and every instance of care occurs in the congregation.

The Third Distinguishing Feature

The third distinguishing feature of pastoral care in congregations involves the relationship between the characters in the case. This feature also may include quite a variety of possibilities corresponding to the possible characters. Case interpreters immediately may be tempted to make psychotherapeutic assumptions about the relationship or relationships, but such assumptions should be resisted. In pastoral care education, the term *relationship* has been a kind of code word associated with psychotherapeutic methods of practicing care. To some, it may bring up contemporary debates on older relationship-centered methods versus newer problem-solving methods. To others, it may point toward the need to move beyond a psychological focus to social, cultural, economic, or political dimensions of relationship. The rush to method and dynamics, however, can cause case readers to bypass the third distinguishing feature of pastoral care in congregations.

In this third feature of case interpretation, it is more important to begin identifying the scope of the relationships between the characters. This is important because it has to do with the sort of experience that pastors and church members may go through as part of a specific Christian community. The scope of the relationship involves two rudimentary things that often have been seen as peripheral in pastoral care education. The first one, mentioned in chapter two, is that the relationship between the pastor and church member may have a history preceding care, may exist outside of care even when care is happening, and may have a future beyond care. For example, one afternoon the senior pastor of a large city congregation steps out of the office and runs into a church member in the hall, and they strike up a conversation. The pastor notices that the church member seems despondent and after sharing this observation hears a troubling story in which the church member admits to being worried about certain things. These two individuals have known each other for years and have been through several momentous events together, from the baptism of the church member's children to the funeral of a parent following a tragic automobile accident. Presently, they serve on a church committee together. Their children attend the same school and sometimes play in each other's homes after school. Their relationship will not end following this care conversation.

The fact that they have a long-term, ongoing relationship of which this specific care situation is only a part gives the second aspect of the scope its significance. This aspect involves the transitions into and out of care that the church member, pastor, and any other case characters have to manage as part of their communal life in the church. Focusing on this transition provides the opportunity to characterize the relationship within care and outside of care and to compare the two. Dealing with this transition in conjunction with the ongoing relationship as it affects care constitutes part of the art of caring in congregations.

The Fourth Distinguishing Feature

As the troubling story unfolds in the conversation between the pastor and despondent church member, the names of other church members are mentioned who are not directly involved in the conversation but who are real factors in it. This is the fourth distinguishing feature, that care in congregations may include discussion about other church members who become part of the care situation. This relates to the complex circumstances unique to the congregational setting mentioned in chapter two, because these are people with whom the minister also has relationships and who also are involved in the church.

In our example, one of the individuals mentioned is the spouse of the despondent church member. It turns out that this spouse has been seeing a psychiatrist for three months and is taking medication for depression. The pastor knows this spouse fairly well but is surprised by the news. Sworn to secrecy by the despondent church member, the pastor must decide how to proceed, but in the meantime the two families are scheduled to have dinner at the church member's home the next evening. Making the transition from care to socializing now presents a challenge to the pastor as well as to the despondent church member.

Another person mentioned is a church member who has a difficult personality and has been a "thorn in the flesh" to the minister for several years. It turns out that on the previous Sunday, during a Sunday school discussion, this other church member made a disparaging remark about psychology, which enraged the church member whose spouse was seeing a psychiatrist. They had argued in the class, and now the minister could very well expect to hear from the difficult church member in the near future. It so happened that the spouse of the difficult church member had been talking to the minister about a possible divorce after six months of what the couple viewed as unsuccessful marriage counseling. Because of the need for confidentiality, the minister could not suggest to the despondent church member that one reason for the disparaging remark about psychology might have been the difficult church member's own therapy experience.

The Fifth Distinguishing Feature

Pastoral care in this situation becomes still more complicated. The minister, the despondent church member, and the difficult church member are embroiled in a heated committee debate over how to spend a large financial gift received from the estate of an elderly church member who died of cancer eleven months ago. This committee factor reveals the fifth distinguishing feature of care in congregations. The minister and church members relate not only to other individual church members who may be mentioned in care but also to organized groups, to the congregation as a whole, and to the community, all of which can be mentioned and become factors in care.

This particular committee has three factions. The despondent church member is in the one that wants to use the money to start a pastoral counseling center. The difficult church member is in the one that wants to put the money toward the development of a shelter for homeless people. The adult grandchild of the deceased church member who gave the money is in the third faction. The pastor cared for the church member who died, and for the surviving family, and knows that the grandchild is grieving. Also, though the deceased church member had refused to designate how the funds were to be used, both the pastor and the grandchild know that the deceased church member often had spoken of refurbishing the church organ. This is what the third faction wants.

Pastors often do not perceive a pastoral care conversation with an individual as a discrete, one-time event. Sometimes such conversations are part of an ongoing care situation involving several people and consisting of a problem or circumstance that may continue for weeks, months, or even years. Accordingly, the conversation with the despondent church member is not seen as a one-time, isolated pastoral care encounter but as part of a larger care situation involving this member and others as they participate in the committee. Now, with the new information about the psychiatric problem of the despondent church member's spouse, it is possible for the minister to see that at least one member of each faction is motivated by personal or family difficulty. The member with the depressed spouse wants a pastoral counseling center. The member facing divorce wants a shelter for homeless people, and the grieving grandchild wants to honor a deceased grandparent by refurbishing the church organ.

The Sixth Distinguishing Feature

The sixth distinguishing feature is that pastoral care in the congregation exists in relation to other aspects of clergy and lay ministry and to the ongoing communal life of the church. Thus, the relational boundaries of pastoral care are porous rather than impervious so that other aspects of ministry and church life can intermingle with care. For instance, the committee containing the three factions includes several aspects of ministry going on simultaneously among those doing the committee work. There is administration of the committee, involving its organization and procedures; there also is care of the committee, with needed attention to its group dynamics as its members relate in potentially hurtful ways because of the factions; there is pastoral care of individual committee members regarding other aspects of their lives that have become intertwined with the committee work; and there is mission in the community concerning how best to spend the money. Hard-and-fast impervious boundaries between pastoral care and other aspects of ministry in the congregation do not exist in this situation or in many others like it.

Reconsidering the First Distinguishing Feature: The Problem

The pastoral care case format requests that the main problem be introduced. Yet what the case author identifies as the main problem may not be what the case interpreter identifies. Even the case author, by the time the case is finished, may see that there is more going on than was realized originally. In the conversation between the pastor and the despondent church member, for instance, the case interpreter may immediately name depression of this church member as the main problem. Yet given the scope of their relationship, the pastor may know the church member well enough to realize that depression is not the problem. Perhaps marital difficulty should be named. Here, however, naming the problem becomes more complicated. The spouse is a church member, too, who also relates to the pastor and who is cared for apart from the marriage. The pastor does not know whether the depression of this spouse is related to the marriage primarily or to something else.

Then, as the case unfolds, the church member with a difficult personality is brought into the picture, which means several things to the pastor. There is the argument between the despondent church member and the difficult church member. Should that be named as the problem? Yet for the pastor, the impending divorce of the difficult church member and the care of that member's spouse is a far more burdensome reality weighing on the pastor's mind. The second thing related to the difficult church member is the committee and its struggle to decide how to spend the money. From the standpoint of the pastor, the problem may very well focus on the committee as seen in relation to the personal and family situations of its members, and the conversation in the hallway outside the pastor's office may be part of the overall care picture. Perhaps the despondent church member would not even have mentioned the argument in the Sunday school class had both the pastor and the despondent church member not been part of the committee discussion.

Or the problem actually may be that of the pastor. It is not enough that the pastor is dealing with one crumbling marriage, bereavement of the grandchild and other family members and friends of the one who died and left the money to the church, and the troublesome committee. Now there is the despondent church member and the spouse who is seeing a psychiatrist for depression, not to mention concern about their marriage and the children. Nor does it stop here. How the church decides to use the money will help set the direction of the church in the community for years to come. Perhaps the pastor is feeling overwhelmed and helpless at having to deal with so many care situations simultaneously. Perhaps the pastor is confused about how to understand the variety of issues being woven together by the circumstances of individuals. Perhaps the pastor is worried about the impact that the committee decision is going to have on the future of the church and community. Or perhaps the pastor is feeling overwhelmed, confused, and worried all at the same time, and this is the problem.

Identifying the facts of the case has a purpose, which is to provide case readers with the information needed to discern a principle contained in those facts. In the next section, a principle for evaluating the facts of the pastoral care case is discussed.

The Principle Contained in the Facts of the Case

Traditionally, the two principles contained in the facts of the case have been method and dynamics, as seen in chapter one. When psychotherapeutic method and a variety of social science dynamics are the principles to be discerned from the facts of the case, the understanding of pastoral care itself is presupposed. In spite of all the expansion of pastoral theology, the phrase *pastoral care and counseling* remains in force as the understanding of pastoral care underlying these two principles. One positive thing about this understanding of pastoral care is that it has emphasized ministry to individuals and families. Yet this understanding has caused care of the congregation to be ignored in pastoral care education, even though suffering of congregations is very real—what is a congregation except a community of people? It has caused lay care to be neglected, and it has a deeply rooted, historical association with outmoded twentieth-century views of ministry that overemphasized pastoral visitation.

It is no longer possible to presuppose an understanding of pastoral care in case interpretation. Instead it is necessary to dig beneath method and dynamics and discover pastoral care anew as the principle contained in the facts of the pastoral care case for the sake of the contemporary church in a changing society.

For discussing pastoral care, we will use a well-known biblical passage, Matthew 25:31–46. This parable envisions the resurrected Jesus on judgment day deciding who will receive an eternal reward and who will receive eternal punishment, like a shepherd separating sheep from goats. The basis for judging is nothing more and nothing less than familiar caring activities, including visiting prisoners, giving a drink to the thirsty, taking care of the sick, feeding the hungry, clothing the naked, and welcoming the stranger. Those who carried out these caring acts are the sheep to be welcomed into the kingdom. Those who failed to care are the goats to be cast into the flames.

The passage begins with Matthew's description of the judgment day scene:

> When the Son of Man comes in his glory, and all the angels with him, then he will sit on the throne of his glory. All the nations will be gathered before him, and he will separate people one from another as a shepherd separates the sheep from the goats, and he will put the sheep at his right hand and the goats at the left. Then the king will say to those at his

right hand, "Come, you that are blessed by my Father, inherit the kingdom prepared for you from the foundation of the world; for I was hungry and you gave me food, I was thirsty and you gave me something to drink, I was a stranger and you welcomed me, I was naked and you gave me clothing, I was sick and you took care of me, I was in prison and you visited me." (Mt. 25:31–36)

The sheep, those at Jesus' right hand, do not recognize having done these things for Jesus:

Then the righteous will answer him, "Lord, when was it that we saw you hungry and gave you food, or thirsty and gave you something to drink? And when was it that we saw you a stranger and welcomed you, or naked and gave you clothing? And when was it that we saw you sick or in prison and visited you?" And the king will answer them, "Truly I tell you, just as you did it to one of the least of these who are members of my family, you did it to me."(vv. 37–40)

Next, Jesus addresses the goats, those at his left hand:

Then he will say to those at his left hand, "You that are accursed, depart from me into the eternal fire prepared for the devil and his angels; for I was hungry and you gave me no food, I was thirsty and you gave me nothing to drink, I was a stranger and you did not welcome me, naked and you did not give me clothing, sick and in prison and you did not visit me." Then they also will answer, "Lord, when was it that we saw you hungry or thirsty or a stranger or naked or sick or in prison, and did not take care of you?" Then he will answer them, "Truly I tell you, just as you did not do it to one of the least of these, you did not do it to me." And these will go away into eternal punishment, but the righteous into eternal life. (vv. 41–46)

One striking thing about this passage is that it places relatively ordinary helping acts within the ultimate setting of judgment and eternity. How does this help us understand pastoral care? In this passage, Jesus is evaluating human beings based on their caring behavior or lack of it. This says to us that caring for others in need is an important christological value that should be made our own.

Pastoral Care Is a Life-Guiding Value

At this level of being a value by which to live, pastoral care is rather like what Edward Farley (1996) calls a deep symbol. He says that deep symbols are "values by which a community understands itself, from which it takes its aims, and to which it appeals as cannons of cultural criticism" (3). Such things as obligation, law, and hope are deep symbols, existing as values undergirding and guiding human life. Farley also calls deep symbols words of power. As words, they exist in enduring "linguistic structures that maintain the community's very existence" (3). They are powerful words because they "empower individuals who live from them and the community that embodies them in narrative and ritual acts" (3).

As an empowering and enduring value, pastoral care provides an ideal, a normative standard for behavior, that summons the Christian community toward a certain direction and away from others. The content of this ideal in the biblical passage is caring for others. Those receiving their eternal reward are those who have responded to specific needs in order to relieve particular kinds of suffering. The hungry are given food. The thirsty are given drink. The stranger is welcomed. The naked are clothed. The sick are taken care of. Prisoners are visited. As an ideal, pastoral care summons us toward those who suffer and encourages us to become more attuned to specific needs of the suffering. It says to us that our actual caring practice should involve responding to the needs of the suffering in our present circumstance, supplying whatever is lacking to ensure relief, recovery, and flourishing. Such needs can exist in individuals, couples, families, and groups, including the church and community. Theologian Sallie McFague (1997), in a wonderfully clear chapter on caring for others, writes: "Christianity…gives preference to certain subjects: the needy…The Christian eye is not just a loving eye, but that eye has a particular slant—it slants toward the oppressed, the poor, the despised, the forgotten" (169).

The christological value of caring for others is not reserved for pastors alone. Rather, anyone who encounters suffering, including the pastor, is to respond. Everyone is among the ones in need at some time or another, and at other times, each should be the one reaching out. This ideal also does not suggest that isolated conversation should be the one and only means of caring for others. Instead, it suggests that many different caring scenarios are possible, requiring different methods as well as knowledge of different kinds of dynamics. Consider feeding the hungry. Seen literally, as one way of caring for the homeless for instance, this caring activity may require the cooperative efforts of many within a congregation, and in some instances the cooperative activity of several congregations, as well as cooperation between congregations and local governments. It even can require attending to environmental concerns (see McFague, 1997, 164–72). At the same time, the spiritually hungry, those hungry for relief from stress, and those hungry for better relationships may need private conversation or a group in which they can begin to tell their stories, solve problems, and reflect on their faith.

Jesus in Solidarity with Those Who Suffer

The Matthew passage also reveals a second christological implication for pastoral care. In his address to the sheep, Jesus does not say that they will inherit the kingdom of heaven because they cared for others as he cared for others. Instead, he says to them that they are to inherit the kingdom because they cared for *him*. They visited *him* when he was in prison, took care of *him* when he was sick, and so forth. Those waiting to receive their reward respond in puzzlement, not having any memory of caring for him, and he answers, "Truly I tell you, just as you did it to one of the least of these who are members of my family, you did it to me" (v. 40). In this christological view of caring for others, Jesus is found standing in solidarity, or in unity, with those in need, identifying with them. They are family, and what is done for one is done for all.

Sigmund Freud (1959) discussed this part of the Matthew passage, verse 40, in his writing on group psychology (26). Freud emphasized the importance of identification, understood as the developmentally earliest expression of an emotional tie between persons, for understanding how the leader of a group relates to the group members and how the group members relate to one another (37–42). Using the church as an example, Freud emphasized Christ's love for the group members as the basis of their love for one another. "There is no doubt that the tie which unites each individual with Christ is also the cause of the tie which unites them with one another" (26). Insofar as this love, or "tie which unites," is an emotional tie, identification is involved, which provides a profound reason for comparing Christianity and family as reflected in verse 40.

In the Matthew passage, the family is a family of sufferers, women and men, young and old, with whom the kingly Jesus identifies. This has a significant implication for a theological understanding of pastoral care. If pastoral care is to be understood christologically, it is not because of those who practice this ministry but instead because of those who suffer and need to receive a caring response.

Pastoral Care Is Fallible

When Jesus addresses the goats, he tells them that they did not care for him, and they respond with the same puzzlement as the sheep. Jesus says to them, "Truly I tell you, just as you did not do it to one of the least of these, you did not do it to me" (v. 45). Pastoral care is vulnerable to neglect because it requires an intentional act. Some people do not respond to the need they see, and others are blind to it. Pastoral care may fail as a normative ideal, not taking root in the life of an individual, group, or church. Or it may be resisted because of the tug of competing values that prevail in contemporary society. In the knowledge of its fallibility and importance, the church must nurture it and keep it alive in a time when values and practices related to caring for others are in danger of atrophy or decline in influence.

Identifying Pastoral Care in the Facts of the Case

Pastoral care as it has just been discussed provides a principle of care that can be used for evaluating the facts of the case described earlier in the chapter, the case involving the pastor, several church members, and the committee trying to decide how to spend money that the church has inherited. The evaluation is the deductive reasoning part of case interpretation that was presented in chapter one. What is of concern in this evaluation is whether it will reveal the principle as contained in the facts of the case. At the end of the evaluation, the principle of care will not be extracted from the discussion any more than a principle of law is extracted from the legal case. If the principle were extracted from the facts of the case, it would mean returning to the conceptual discussion of pastoral care in the previous section in light of what was gained from evaluating the facts of the case. This might lead to further conceptual development of pastoral care and have implications for practice depending on what was learned in the evaluation. There is another direction, though, that can be taken following the evaluation, a direction that has a direct implication for learning to practice pastoral care more effectively in the congregational setting. This direction will be taken in the next chapter on case interpretation. The matter at hand, however, is evaluating the facts of the case.

Pastoral care as a christological value can be seen initially in the pastor's willingness to talk to the despondent church member on the spot without prior notice. Perhaps the person needs for the pastor to listen, and that will be enough. Yet if pastoral care is providing an ideal that summons us toward those who suffer and encourages us to become attuned to their needs, it is not possible to stop with the surface of the conversation outside the pastor's office door.

As the conversation unfolds, the pastor begins to perceive the suffering of several other church members, including that of the depressed spouse of the despondent church member, the troubling church member who is facing divorce, and the spouse who wants the divorce. This spouse had been talking to the pastor previously. Then, when the pastor puts the conversation with the despondent church member in the larger context of the committee with three factions, the perception of suffering expands further. There are the adult grandchild's bereavement and the potential suffering of the committee members if the factions become contentious. There is also the need in the local community to which two factions in the committee want to respond by developing either a counseling center or shelter for the homeless.

The pastor is in the position of being aware of more suffering than can be responded to personally, yet the mandate of the caring ideal is to respond. This can make pastors feel as if they are in a bind, because pastoral care often does not happen one situation at a time. In the case being examined, it is important to recognize that the pastor is not the only one who is aware of the suffering or responding to it. The despondent church member is caring for the depressed spouse, who also is receiving professional psychiatric care. The divorcing couple has been receiving marriage counseling, though it has failed. The committee members are working on possible ways for the congregation to respond to suffering in the community, and they may come up with a creative plan. If they do, it will involve still other church members, not merely the pastor. The grieving grandchild has the support of family and friends and takes solace from the choir's singing and the organist's playing in worship. None of these situations will be resolved immediately, and the pastor will have opportunities for contact with most of these church members and some people in the community over time. Yet it is those who participate in the church community who will respond for the relief of suffering.

Can Jesus be seen standing in solidarity with all the suffering people? Sometimes it seems not, especially when caring acts are very practical and nothing explicitly religious emerges. In the biblical passage, however, Matthew argues strongly that even the most practical caring act, such as giving a drink to the thirsty, is most highly valued and is inherently religious. It points to where Jesus is, standing in unity with those who suffer. In this sense of solidarity, Jesus is with each of the married couples and their children, with the grieving adult grandchild, with the needy in the community, even with the overwhelmed pastor in the pastor's own need. The type of caring act is not what determines its religious significance, but rather, what matters is whether it hits the mark by addressing actual need and relieving suffering. Whether care involves standing in a church hallway and listening to a troubled soul or sitting in a committee deciding how to use funds to meet the needs of suffering people in the community, care is in the service of those with whom Christ stands.

This raises the question of whether the pastor in the case hit the mark in caring for troubled church members. When the pastor was seeing the suffering people in terms of a series of individuals, each needing a response, care seemed to be an impossible task. Realizing that others also care could help relieve the pastor's suffering, but there is an additional opportunity for the pastor. The pastoral care situations that the pastor is experiencing exist in relation to other aspects of ministry and intermingle with them, as seen in the sixth distinguishing feature of pastoral care discussed earlier. This interrelationship was discussed in terms of the different facets of the committee, such as administration, group dynamics, and care of the individuals all going on simultaneously, but the view of the pastor does not stop there.

The pastor has the opportunity to see the multiple instances of suffering, taken together as a whole, in relation to other aspects of the church community. This opportunity provides an occasion for the pastor's reflection. For instance, the pastor may wonder, How is this suffering going on in our midst right now having an impact on my ministry and on the congregation? It may, for instance, be influencing the meaning of worship and preaching for the pastor. Individual encounters with the suffering people may be sporadic, but the worship service is the one place where the pastor may have contact with all the suffering church members on a regular weekly basis for months on end. This gives the pastor a unique opportunity for care by seeing worship and preaching as one way that the church responds to the needs of the sufferers. This does not mean naively targeting a sermon at someone (who is guaranteed not to show up that Sunday, as new pastors soon discover). Rather, it has to do with such things as worship's tone, content, style, and sensitivity to those who worship. It assumes that those who suffer need to worship God and that worship leaders should strive to make the worship service a place where this can happen.

Finally, are there any goats in the facts of this case? First, the pastor may feel neglectful, but the reality of this should be judged according to the circumstances. For instance, if the pastor is the only one to practice care, and church members are not seen as caring also, the pastor may not only feel in a bind but also have a self-perception of neglecting pastoral care. Second, personal suffering may prevent some committee members from enabling the church to care for the community. This can be seen in the three factions' struggle to decide how to spend the money. For instance, personal grief rather than the actual need of the church or community is motivating the grandchild of the one who gave the money to influence the committee to recommend refurbishing the church organ. Grief is making it difficult for the grandchild to see the need of others in the church and community right now. Third, the despondent and troublesome church members also are motivated by their personal situations, but those situations permit them to be more in accord with the church's opportunity to care for the community, whether the money were used for a pastoral counseling center or for a homeless shelter. Still, because of their own situations, they potentially could undermine the committee effort by being too rigid and not displaying the openness and flexibility the committee needs to move ahead fruitfully.

This last characteristic of pastoral care, its fallibility, has a whole other dimension today. Beyond the various dynamics of those who participate in the ministry of care, changes in the contemporary world are revealing the vulnerability of care and the possibility that it may decline in power and effectiveness. Therefore, in the final section, the fallibility of care will be discussed in more detail.

The Atrophy of Pastoral Care

It is common today for people to talk about how the world is changing and how these changes affect different parts of contemporary society, such as business practices, cultural values, and religious institutions. Pastoral care does not escape being affected by a changing world. Pastoral theologians have begun discussing this in terms of postmodernism and pastoral care, but it is a discussion far from concluded. Farley (1996) has a particular take on postmodernism in relation to its effects on deep symbols. He is concerned with a profound historical shift that is ushering in a new cultural epoch. "As a term, 'postmodern' has many meanings…As a term for the historical shift, the rise of a new epoch, it names a liberation into plurality (from provincialism), relativity (from absolutisms), and difference (from the old frozen authorities). At the same time it describes the void and anxiety we experience when our very selves are dispersed, bureaucratized, isolated, and rendered autonomous" (12). This profound historical shift, with its effects on culture and human beings, places deep symbols in a precarious position: "If we do live in a cultureless society, if we do experience a dispersed consciousness, if there is no overall inscription mediated to us, surely that will affect the words of power. In such a situation how can we remember, employ, think, or be shaped by the words of power?" (12).

In the postmodern world that Farley describes, pastoral care is subject to the same atrophy, or decline, as deep symbols. In language, pastoral care may be weakened as its meaning is eroded and as the terms associated with it no longer convey its religious connection. Then pastoral care becomes cut off from its christological aspects. We saw in chapter one that in the 1930s Boisen, Cabot, and Dicks were witnessing the decline of a historic name for pastoral care called the *cure of souls,* which was abandoned in favor of more contemporary language. Even though Cabot used the term *growth of souls,* it was Dicks's phrase *pastoral work* that survived. But even the modern-sounding term *work* from the nineteenth century did not last. It took many years for *pastoral care and counseling* terminology to emerge and become established in the mid-twentieth century, but none of its terms convey anything similar to the poetic and spiritual depth of the *cure of souls.*

In what Farley calls the interhuman sphere, pastoral care faces its most poignant challenge. The interhuman sphere has to do with intimate, personal relations at a primordial level.

> This sphere is neither a collection of individuals nor an institutional structure. The relation that forms over the years between mother and child, wife and husband, friend and friend, is not reducible to the psychological dynamics of each individual nor is it a social institution. It is irreducibly itself. This relation can be violated, betrayed, deepened, or

renewed. It can have certain qualities such as love, competitiveness, or guilt. (21)

For his understanding of how the interhuman is formed, Farley draws on the philosophy of Emmanuel Levinas:

> It is formed by what Emmanuel Levinas calls the vulnerable face, which draws the individual out of its natural egocentricity into relation. The interhuman is already formed and in place by the time an infant or child becomes a self-conscious individual. And, it is always, already there and in place when social organizations are created and human enterprises become institutionalized (21).

The interhuman sphere, says Farley, gives deep symbols their power to function in human life because they are created in this sphere. Postmodern society may have a negative impact on the interhuman sphere when it is suppressed within societal institutions and when it is excluded from them. Farley seems to be saying that society's institutions influence contemporary people so pervasively that they provide substitutes for intimate communities that nurture the interhuman sphere and deep symbols, and as a result contemporary individuals lose touch with the "vulnerable face" and with mutually supportive relationships. A stark example comes from sexuality and family life. "Such a society will develop a faceless sexuality with minimum mutual responsibility, a family life whose only staying power is the passions that initially swept the individuals into marriage and the endless subsequent negotiations for rights and powers, with the result that it has little power to endure over time. The family...bereft of the face and the words of power, becomes an environment of alienated intimacy" (22).

Ironically, pastoral care education may have contributed to the decline of pastoral care by shifting the teaching and learning of care to two societal institutions, including medical centers and the psychotherapy office associated with the mental health industry. By learning the ministry of care in these settings, pastors are separated from the congregation, the community whose relationships and traditions exist in no small measure to engender and nurture the value and practice of caring for others. Medical and psychotherapeutic institutions supply alternative caring practices not associated with relationships in congregations, and they provide alternative views of church members as patients and clients. It can seem as if there is nothing much left for the Christian faith to do in the realm of pastoral care except to justify these alternatives through the interdisciplinary dialogue between theology and psychology.

Contemporary calls for pastoral care and counseling to move beyond the so-called counseling model of care have opened the door to a closer focus on religious practices and congregations in pastoral care education. Still, this focus is from a distance. Moving beyond counseling often seems to mean placing pastoral care within the social sciences, and therefore within academe, where social scientists study such things as the church with scientific methods. Care in pastoral care education remains as displaced from its church community as ever. The clinical institutions still provide most method, but the academically based social sciences are changing the view of the church member in the sense that the causes of suffering are being widened to include all the dimensions of life that correspond to all the different social sciences.

Finally, in contemporary society pastoral care also may suffer atrophy from within the church, as many religious communities are shaken to the core, being reduced to struggles for survival in a society that can seem increasingly strange and unfamiliar. Farley puts it well when he writes, "Christian communities now live in the very face of difference: different religious faiths, different ethnic traditions, different social behaviors that would have shocked and appalled our Victorian forebears" (17). In the "face of difference," churches can be tempted to develop a circling-the-wagons mentality for survival, not only survival of the particular congregation but of old ways. Such a mentality is detrimental to building relationships in the church community that engender and nurture the care of others.

Farley says that in the face of difference the Christian symbols survive, but they become like tunes that cannot quite be remembered:

> The tune is there. We would recognize it if someone else whistled it. But for the moment, the tune is only there in our memory bouncing among other tunes...Recall the pathos of one of Israel's exiled poets. I paraphrase the poet's cry. In this strange land, a land that is not ours, a land without any fixed place of the Lord's presence, the temple, a land whose stories are not our stories, a land of strange armies, rulers, customs, and languages, how can we sing the Lord's song? Can we only put away our musical instruments and try not even to recall the tune? In very different historical circumstances, the Christian movement in the industrialized West

is experiencing something like that. Its words of power are tunes it cannot quite recall. (25)

Many churches, attempting to "sing the Lord's song" as well as they can, are forging into unknown territory. Their clergy and members are learning to reorganize themselves at congregational and higher judicatory levels as they cast off bloated, hierarchical, stagnant church bureaucracies from the past. They are learning to identify, appreciate, and reach out to younger generations. They are embracing mission in the community, which is becoming more dependent on the efforts of local congregations. They are wrestling with prickly generational differences within congregations. They are learning to live among all kinds of people in society. Although pastoral care suffers decline in a transitional society, it surely remains active as an ideal summoning churches into a future filled with divine mystery.

4

Learning from Pastoral Care
Case Interpretation

Encountering meaning that comes from a pastoral care case enables case readers to learn more about their own pastoral care in the congregational setting. This may seem obvious if the reader is the one who wrote the case. Then the case author has the advantage of having experienced the actual pastoral care about which the case is written as well as the advantage of having written the case. In pastoral care education, a whole class may focus on the case presented by the author and contribute to the learning of that person. As valuable as this may be for the case author, it also raises a question. What about the rest of the class members' learning? It would seem remarkably inefficient if, during the course of a semester, students could learn only during the presentation of their own cases.

We affirm in this chapter that a pastoral care case contains an educational possibility not only for the case writer but also for others. Someone who reads a case written by someone else has neither the benefit of experiencing the actual pastoral care about which the case is written nor the benefit of writing the case. Nevertheless, readers of cases written by others can learn more about their own pastoral care through case interpretation.

Learning from Cases Written by Others

Typically, the first reading of a pastoral care case involves just sitting down and reading through the case to become familiar with it. Some combination of understanding and misunderstanding occurs, and questions about its meaning may arise. Hmm...I wonder what that means? Why did she say that? What's going on with those people? It may be helpful to write down your questions. Then a second reading becomes more analytical as the interpreter reads through the case for the purpose of (1) identifying the facts of the case and (2) discerning its principle. "Let's see, the first distinguishing feature is..." This analysis also can be written down. Finally, there is a kind of third reading that is the reader's own self-interpretation in light of the case meaning disclosed through the analytical reading. It is, in a sense, the flip side of the second analytical reading, and it too can be written down.

This self-interpretation of the reader involves what Paul Ricoeur calls appropriation, which means that the reader begins to "make one's own" the possibilities being disclosed in case meaning. Ricoeur also calls the meaning coming from the text through interpretation "the world of the text" (1981, 182–93). These possibilities being disclosed are foreign to the reader before being encountered in the interpretation, but now they are being claimed as the reader's own, or appropriated. In pastoral care case interpretation, appropriation means that as the reader encounters the case meaning, a new possibility for actual pastoral care may arise for the reader.

Appropriation is Ricoeur's name for what the philosopher Hans-Georg Gadamer (1975) calls application. Gadamer says that applying textual meaning to the reader's life is not something that comes after interpretation and after gaining understanding of a text. Instead, application is an inherent part of interpretation and understanding: "In the course of our reflections we have come to see that understanding always involves something like the application of the text to be understood to the present situation of the interpreter" (274). This says to pastoral care case readers that learning from cases not their own is a genuine possibility. It also suggests that cases other than ones written by students can be used in a class or in a group.

During the course of an interview, Ricoeur was asked about this part of interpretation, and in response he, with the interviewer, set out the main features of application, or appropriation (Mario J. Valdes, 1991, 491–96). The first thing to realize in appropriation is that there is more than one possible interpretation of a case, just as there is more than one possible interpretation of a biblical passage, a poem, or a historical event. Because there is more than one possible interpretation, judgment becomes an important feature of appropriation. If there is going to be anything to appropriate, the reader must use judgment, or make decisions, about the meaning being disclosed. For instance, sometimes this involves deciding which of two different possible interpretations seems more convincing. Other times, it involves choosing to focus on one part of the meaning that seems particularly pertinent and letting the other part go for the time being.

In a sense, judgment closes off further interpretation, but the second feature of appropriation balances this closure with a continuing openness, the openness of the reader's imagination. For many years, Ricoeur has emphasized the role of imagination in appropriation, and he describes it as the "imaginative variations of the ego" (Valdes, 1991, 494). Using imagination frees the reader not only to identify with different characters and situations in the case but also to envision the possibilities within the reader's own actual ministry of pastoral care. For example, let's say that the reader is a pastor who always has assumed that pastoral care has a very narrow scope, confined to private conversation between the pastor and church member. When the pastor has named a family undergoing tragedy in a pastoral prayer during worship, or has worked behind the scenes administratively to help start a ministry to the poor in the local community, such things have seemed outside the scope of official pastoral care. However, as a result of imaginatively encountering case meaning through interpretation, the pastor begins to get the idea that pastoral care may have a much larger scope. Ministry seems less splintered as the pastor begins perceiving, or acknowledging, connections between personal care conversations and more public ministry to the congregation, as well as caring involvement of church members. Diverse activities all begin to fall within the scope of care. Now a new question may arise concerning its limits.

Through judgment and imagination, case readers apply possibilities emerging from case meaning to themselves and their own pastoral care, but there are constraints. Normally, case interpretation does not happen in a vacuum. Rather, it happens most often in the context of pastoral care education programs, which provide a whole tradition of case interpretation. This tradition, or this history of case interpretation, provides checks or boundaries and guidelines that may help keep case interpretation on a positive and fruitful course that has the most chance of being helpful to students. For instance, case discussion in groups affords case readers the opportunity to hear the judgment and imagination of other readers and to submit their own judgment and imagination to the collective wisdom of the group and of the interpretive tradition conveyed by the teacher.

Appropriation is the culmination of pastoral care case interpretation. If case interpretation proceeds by identifying the facts of the case and discerning the principle contained in those facts, it comes to fruition as the case meaning becomes relevant for the actual pastoral care of the reader.

Presenting a Pastoral Care Case: The First Reading

One day a pastor and I (Gene Fowler) were talking about pastoral care, and our conversation turned to instances of care other than private conversation between the pastor and church member. She told me about a ministry experience as an example, and I asked her to write it down as a pastoral care case. She did not have the advantage of reading the chapters of this book (some were not yet written). Nevertheless, she agreed to tell this story of pastoral care using the basic categories of the pastoral care case format found in chapter two. This case is the telling of her pastoral care story, though names and places are changed.

As the pastor of a congregation, I will be reading this case that I did not write with an eye toward appropriation. I am wagering that through my encounter with the case, something will emerge as a possibility for my own pastoral care. At the end of the case, I will make a few comments that strike me as I read through it, and then I will proceed to the second reading.

Title: The Empty Bag

Introduction

This is my first year out of seminary. My name is Kathy Johnson, and I am a twenty-six-year-old woman who has become the associate pastor of Small River Presbyterian Church (U.S.A.). One of my primary responsibilities is working with the youth at this church. On the last weekend in April, I led the annual weekend youth retreat at the local Presbyterian church camp, and it was during the retreat that pastoral care with Robert occurred. As I planned the retreat program, I chose the theme "The Me I Want to Be" with an eye toward the high school seniors near graduation. Our Saturday afternoon session, which lasted one hour, included ten teenagers and three adults in addition to me. In this session, each teenager was to talk about someone respected or admired, a role model for "the me I want to be." I had expected to hear about sports figures, musicians, and actors, but instead I heard quite a bit about parents. Then came Robert's turn to speak. Obviously affected by the stories his peers were telling, especially those about fathers, his own story about his troubled relationship with his father and stepmother came spilling out along with his tears. This was not a continuation of the group exercise. Instead, it became the confession of a suffering young man that called for a caring response. This case is about Robert and how several teens, an adult adviser, and I cared for him.

The Congregational Setting

Robert is a member of Small River Presbyterian Church (U.S.A.). The senior pastor, John Marshall, is in his eighth year there. Based on my relatively brief experience with this congregation over nine months, I would say that the congregation seems very committed to the Reformed tradition and tends to describe its theology accordingly. As I have experienced it so far, the congregation strongly emphasizes Christ as the Word of God, the proclamation of this Word in worship, and the study of the Bible educationally. Corresponding to this theological emphasis is a focus on local and global mission, seen as an important expression of Christian service.

The congregation is over two hundred years old and has approximately eight hundred members. It is located in Small River, a town of ten thousand bordering other small towns in a large suburban sprawl approximately twenty miles from a large city. Traditionally, the congregation has contained a mix of white-collar and blue-collar families, a mix that seems to appeal to the many middle-class people in the local community. For many years, the church members were all Caucasian. Now, approximately 3 percent are African American, and 2 percent are Asian American. This shift reflects changing demographics in Small River and the surrounding area. The shift is also an important part of growth in the congregation. Five years ago, fully 50 percent of the congregation was retirement age. Now, a growing percentage of young and middle-aged adults make up a congregation that slowly is becoming racially and culturally pluralistic.

When I first talked to the church committee about the associate pastor position, they gave me some information about the youth group. Last year, some incidents in the youth group brought a strong reaction from some parents and other church members. I do not know many details, and I do not know about each incident, but the two I do know about are enough to explain why church members became concerned. The first involved alcohol and marijuana use at a youth group Valentine dance. The second occurred at the annual spring youth retreat. There was drinking, drug use, and sex at the retreat. Most youth involved in these and other similar incidents last year were high school seniors who graduated and would not be in the group this year. I accepted the position knowing the situation, and I don't mind saying that it made me more than a little anxious. Not only would I have the responsibility of making sure that this year was different, but the congregation also would be monitoring the situation closely. Looking back, I am beginning to see that when I accepted the position, I stepped into what I now think was a complicated pastoral care situation involving several teens in the youth group. They were young church members engaging in inappropriate and potentially destructive behaviors. The situation impacted many people directly, including each individual teenager in the group, last year's interim associate pastor, and adult youth advisers. Then there were the parents of each teen, the pastor, the Christian Education Committee, and the congregation. How could the church respond in a caring way to these teens? Did some parents also need pastoral care? Who exactly should or could do the actual responding? How was all this related to other facets of ministry and church life in which I was to be involved?

The Pastoral Care Participants

The Youth Group

I was thrown into a difficult situation, and I had to figure out how to respond, without any assurance that the results would be positive. Fortunately, my response did have positive results. Very early in the year, we had a youth group lock-in at the church. In preparation for this event, I did something that set the tone for the rest of our time together. I simply told the group that there could be no sex, drugs, or drinking at the lock-in or at any youth group meeting. If there were, parents would be called automatically and immediately. I was pleasantly surprised when they accepted these rules without question, and they actually seemed relieved (undoubtedly, some of the relief was really mine). This also seemed to be the thing that established trust between us, a trust that grew during the course of the year. Since the group got off to a good start and continued in a positive direction rather than reverting to last year's behavior, the stage was set for the spring retreat to be the kind of event in which pastoral care could happen as it did. It became possible for group members to care for one another. The pastoral care participants who responded to Robert were Kim, John, Bill, and Jane, who were youth group members; Jay, who was one of the three adult advisers; and me.

Robert

Robert, an eighteen-year-old high school senior, is tall and exceptionally slender. He tends to be concerned with his appearance, and other kids tease him because he blushes easily when the topic turns to dating, sex, or his height. He is good-natured, with a sense of humor, but he sometimes resorts to silliness or goofiness. Others take this in stride, but they will call him on it if he gets too extreme. Robert is not in a steady dating relationship, and I do not know whether he dates at all.

Robert lives at home with his parents and has an older sister, Margaret, who graduated from high school last year and is now in college. Their mother, Grace, died of cancer when Robert was five. His father, Alfred, remarried three years after his wife's death, when Robert was eight. The father and stepmother, Mary, then had two children, who became Robert's half brother and half sister. They are Ben, who is five, and Julie, who is seven. The senior pastor told me that Mary clearly favors her children over Robert and his sister and that the father does not tend to intervene when there is conflict between Robert and Mary. The senior pastor also told me that Robert and his family have lived in Small River, and even in the same house, for Robert's entire life. Before Grace's death, the whole family attended Small River Presbyterian Church regularly. When Alfred remarried, the parents began participating in church only sporadically while sending the children weekly. I have not had any contact with the family.

My relationship with Robert began nine months ago, when I started my ministry with the youth group. He has attended our weekly group meetings faithfully, only missing occasionally when he was required to baby-sit his half brother and half sister. In the group, I have experienced him as a little hyperactive, and I have had to call his attention back to the task at hand periodically. However, this has not been a major problem by any means. The other teens seem to like him and appreciate his sense of humor. We have not had many private conversations during the year, and he has seemed shy in the few times we have talked. Although he has hinted at family difficulties from time to time in the group, it was a real surprise to me when he disclosed his feelings about his family at the retreat.

What Happened

We arrived at the retreat on Friday evening and had an introductory group session followed by a campfire. The next morning, we met for our second group session, and after lunch we had our third. In preparation for this Saturday afternoon session, I had instructed each group member to put in a paper bag something that symbolized a person whom the group member admired or respected. It was to be the visual representation of a role model for "the me I want to be." In this group session, we were to share what we had put in our bags. After lunch, the group sat under a tree in a circle and one by one shared what was in each one's bag. Because the group included teenagers, three adult advisers, and me, we did not have much opportunity in the one-hour session to discuss what each person shared. Nevertheless, the process seemed to unfold in an unrushed manner as each group member described what was in the bag that he or she had brought, who the object represented, and what impact that person had had on "the me I want to be." As I mentioned in the introduction, I had expected that some role models would include professional athletes, rock stars, and actors, but I was in for a surprise. Parents, other family members, and teachers were the ones that these teens were looking to as role models. I found myself pleased that the group had taken the assignment seriously. The hour progressed, and there were only a few of us left to speak.

Kim opened her bag and brought out a necklace she had received as a gift from her aunt. She talked about her aunt, saying, "She's always interested in what I'm doing and what I think.

"She encourages me to do my best at whatever I do. She trusts my judgment, and she really listens to me. When I'm an adult, I want to be to someone else what she is to me." When she finished saying this about her aunt, she simply sat silently, indicating that she was finished and that it was time for the next person to speak.

John said that he would go next and brought out of his bag a book belonging to his father, a professor. He said, "Up until the past couple of months, I haven't understood my dad at all, and we really were not getting along very well. But I've been watching him, and I see some things for the first time, like how he chooses to spend his time with us, like how he reads to us at the dinner table and prays with us. And, up until a few weeks ago, I really hated that."

I wondered what had happened a couple of months ago to change John's perception of his dad, but I did not say anything as he continued speaking. "I've also noticed how when he's really disappointed in me, he doesn't yell or anything but sits down with me and talks real quiet about what his expectations are of me and about what his hopes are for me. He's working real hard to get me ready to make my own decisions, and I really respect that. I see how he's living his values all the time, and I think, 'Wow, I hope I can be a father like him.'"

The group members sat quietly as a reflective mood seemed to overtake the group. Next, I opened my bag and took out a wooden jewelry box that my father had made for me and that represented him. As I was bringing out the jewelry box, I said to Kim, "Do you remember the night you asked me about my call to ministry, and I said it was a long story and that I would find time to tell you later? I want you to know that I didn't forget."

After hearing all these stories about parents, and after having spent time thinking about my father, my emotions were coming to the surface. I felt some tears welling up in me as I said to Kim and the group, "My call had a lot to do with my dad, who committed suicide five years ago this weekend." I talked about my father's quiet faith and how it was expressed through his participation in my home church, and then I shared with them what a male friend had told me once about my father. I said, "A guy my age told me that my father had made him feel so great when he joined the choir as a teenager. He said my dad had talked to him every week at rehearsal, asking him how he was doing and how school was going. It was such a little thing, but it really made him feel that somebody cared about him."

Then I talked briefly about how my grief following my father's death opened my eyes to the suffering of others and to the thought that I could respond to suffering people by being with them and helping them. "That was the beginning of my call, I think, and I find that I look for ways to bring what I learned from my dad with me into my ministry."

Kim reached over and, touching my shoulder, said, "I didn't want to pry when I asked you." I responded, "I wanted to tell you, but I knew I couldn't do it without crying." When Kim touched my shoulder and said what she did, I experienced her caring for me through her gentleness. Imagine that, a church member, a teenager no less, caring for the pastor. What I did not know then, but was about to find out momentarily, was how capable these young church members were of caring.

Following another moment of silence, the last person in the group left to speak, Robert, said, "My bag is empty. I couldn't think of what to bring, of who I wanted to be. I was hoping I would find something here but I didn't. But now, hearing you talk about the people who mean so much to you, I realize that I don't have anyone like that in my life."

Robert looked down, blushing, and then he continued, "John, when you talk about your dad, I feel so bad because I would give anything to have my dad care about me like that. You guys know that since my dad got married again he hasn't had much time for me. It's always, 'Mary needs me,' or 'your brother and sister are little and really need my time.' The only time he ever starts a conversation with me is to tell me what a screwup I am. And her, Mary, I feel her watching me, biding her time, waiting for me to leave home so that they won't ever have to think about me again. I used to think she must have come from a Nazi family. She was always issuing orders: 'Ja wohl, Frau Kommandant!'" Robert saluted sharply as he said this and then finished what he was saying. "I can't wait to get away from her. That's why I've enlisted in the Navy so I can get away from them. And maybe there I'll find someone who is 'the me I want to be.'"

Looking down at his lap once more, Robert started to cry softly. Jay, one of the adult lay leaders, was sitting next to Robert and put his arm around him. The others were quiet. Robert continued, "Maybe they're right. Maybe I really am just a screwup. I sure haven't set this town on fire."

I was listening so intently to Robert that I was a little startled when Kim responded to him, saying, "Robert, I know how hard they are on you, but you are so much more than you're seeing through them! You are one of the nicest guys I know. I'm glad you're my friend."

Bill picked up on what Kim was saying and chimed in, "Robert, we've been through a lot together. People have laughed at us and mocked us, but I don't care anymore. When everyone else was saying I was just a geek, you were willing to be seen with me and with Jane."

Then Jane, who often talks nonstop, spoke. "Robert, we've been in the same Sunday school class for twelve years, and you are the only one who has never said a mean word to me. Maybe that should be part of the 'me I want to be.'"

Robert did not respond to those who had just spoken. Instead, he straightened up, looked at me, and said, "When you talked about your dad bringing people from the outside into the center of the group, that really got to me. This church, this group, this year, has been the only place I ever felt on the inside. Do you know that no matter what goofy thing I've said or done as I was coming in, you've always been happy to see me?" He looked around the circle, "All of you, you've been glad to see me."

Before I could respond, Albert, a very quiet sophomore, said, "Not me!" Everyone laughed.

After the laughter stopped, John said, "Robert, I know I'm lucky to have my dad, but I'm glad that you have this group and the church because we really do care about you. And if we care about you so much, then God must care about you a whole lot more."

I did not wait to hear how Robert might have responded to John. Instead, I asked Robert, "Is that something you can take with you, that we care about you and that God cares even more about you? Because it's true." Robert nodded and smiled.

I continued, "The 'me I want to be' is already in you in many ways. I'll be hoping and praying that you'll discover it and know in your heart how much God loves that 'me,' because this many people can't be wrong!"

Kim walked over to Robert and gave him a hug, as did many of the others, including me. We had gone over the allotted hour, and it was time for the group session to end. The rest of the afternoon would be spent playing, and a spirit of kindness and encouragement seemed to pervade the group for the rest of the day.

(Comments from a first reading: First, the themes of identity and grief seem to be prominent for Robert and for the pastor. Second, the experience under the tree seems gracious, for Robert and for the group as a whole. Third, I am mindful that in the congregation, pastoral care often arises unexpectedly in the midst of other things.)

Case Evaluation: The Second Reading

For this reading, I will follow the traditional interpretive procedure found in the case method of teaching, which begins with identifying the facts of the case and then moves to discerning the principle contained in them. I will not try to go as deeply as possible into each aspect of this procedure, but instead will touch on each part in order to present an overall picture of it. For identifying the facts of the case, I will draw on the scope of pastoral care with its six distinguishing features.

Facts of the Case

1. The first distinguishing feature of pastoral care in the congregational setting involves the pastoral care situation, or the problem, being addressed in the case.

One pastoral care situation in this case involves the youth group as a whole. Recall Pastor Johnson's observation in the second section of the case that being hired at Small River Presbyterian Church was like entering into a complex pastoral care situation. The church does not want the inappropriate behavior of the youth group during the previous year to be repeated.

The second situation is the bereavement of Pastor Johnson due to her father's suicide, seen in relation to her identity as a pastor. Although the case is not written in order for her to address her suffering, it does come out in the case when she cries during her discussion about her father. Her bereavement does not prevent her from having a positive ministry to the youth group.

The third pastoral care situation is the one that Pastor Johnson names in the introduction. It involves Robert. When it comes time for Robert to share what is in his bag with the group, he is put in an embarrassing position because he has nothing in the bag. The object in the bag is supposed to represent the "me I want to be," or a role model for an adult identity. Robert's problem is that he has no role model, which seems to reflect a struggle with his identity. As his story unfolds, the problem of the empty bag leads to his revealing the difficult relationship he has with his parents. He portrays himself as neglected by his father and unwanted by his stepmother.

2. The second distinguishing feature involves the characters found in the case.

The characters are Robert, Pastor Johnson, the youth group, and the youth advisers. Youth group members named are Kim, John, Bill, Jane, and Albert. The one youth adviser named is Jay. This leaves four youth group members and two adult advisers who are present at the retreat but not named.

3. The third distinguishing feature involves the relationships between the characters. Because there are so many people involved in this case, there are many relationships. Some of them revolve around Robert. He relates to Pastor Johnson, the youth group as a whole, the adult advisers, specific group members who respond to him during the meeting, and Jay, who comforts him when he cries. Other relationships between characters revolve around Pastor Johnson. She relates to the youth group as a whole, to Kim, and to Robert.

Pastor Johnson gave some background on her relationship with the youth group. From the beginning the relationship was tinged with anxiety because the church, a new and first church for her, was looking over her shoulder, wanting her to prevent the youth group from going in the direction of the previous year. Over the course of the year, trust developed between her and the youth group as boundaries were set and accepted. She says very little about her relationships with individual youth group members or advisers. She and Robert spoke only a few times, and even then there was not much to say. Also, Kim had asked her about her call to ministry, and she had declined to talk about it until the retreat. We don't know what families of youth group members she interacted with in other areas of church life, but it seems reasonable to assume that there must have been some interaction between Pastor Johnson and some family members of the youth.

What would the future hold for all these relationships in light of the pastoral care experienced at the retreat? The high school seniors in the youth group would be going their separate ways. Assuming, for instance, that Robert really was planning to join the Navy after graduation, he no longer would be at Small River Presbyterian Church. Younger members, however, would be back next year. What was their experience of the group, and how did the care affect them? How would planning for next year's youth group be different for the pastor?

4. The fourth distinguishing feature is that pastoral care in congregations may include discussion about other church members, who become part of the pastoral care situation.

Because of the exercise with the bags, many family members of the group were discussed. Kim discussed her aunt, and John discussed his father. Pastor Johnson discussed her father, but he is deceased and was never a member of the congregation. Robert discussed his family, including his deceased biological mother, his father, his stepmother, his older sister, and his younger half brother and half sister. Because the family hardly ever is seen at church, and because the pastor is so new, it is not surprising that she does not know Robert's family. Yet as Robert's younger half brother and half sister come into the youth program, new opportunities may very well arise for her to get to know them. Her experience with Robert now becomes part of her history, and her newfound knowledge of the family can inform her in potential future ministry with the family. A year or two down the road, it could be interesting and meaningful for her to hear what Robert's parents have to say about their relationship with him.

5. The fifth distinguishing feature involves relating the pastoral care situation to organized groups and to the congregation as a whole, all of which can be mentioned and may become factors in pastoral care.

Pastor Johnson first discussed the congregation as a whole. In the second section of the case, "The Congregational Setting," she gave a brief overview of the church. Next she provided information about being hired at the church and about last year's youth group, indicating that the youth group situation was a concern to the church community. Here, the part of the church to which she is relating is the search committee that interviewed her and told her about the youth group. This leads to the question of her relationship to the congregation in the present. Because it was impossible to escape a comparison with the previous year, there was pressure on the pastor for the youth group to do well during the present year and at the retreat. One or more of the adult advisers might even be reporting to other church members on the success of the retreat. How was the retreat going to be viewed by parents, the senior pastor, the Christian Education Committee, and by the congregation as a whole? Would it be a sign showing that youth ministry at Small River Presbyterian Church had turned around and was going in a healthier direction?

6. The sixth distinguishing feature is that pastoral care in the congregation exists in relation to other aspects of ordained and lay ministry and to the ongoing communal life of the church.

This distinguishing feature brings out the need of Pastor Johnson and the youth group to walk a line between Christian education and pastoral care during the group meeting under the tree at the retreat. When Pastor Johnson shared what was in her bag and became tearful as she talked about her father, Kim and the group as a whole had to respond in some way. A caring response was called for because Pastor Johnson was disclosing her suffering to them. Yet the suffering and caring response remained within the context of the educational exercise. Then, when Robert began to speak, he too continued the Christian education exercise, while at the same time introducing his suffering related to his relationship with his parents. If what Robert said about his parents had been spoken during a private conversation with Pastor Johnson, it easily could have been seen as pastoral care verbatim material. What Robert said generated caring responses from the group members, and this put Pastor Johnson in the position of having to continue leading the group while at the same time not prohibiting the group members from responding to Robert. She could not have predicted this sudden shift into an explicit pastoral care situation, nor did she have the opportunity to segregate pastoral care and Christian education neatly into different slots.

Discerning the Principle of Pastoral Care

In the deductive part of interpreting the pastoral care case, the principle to be used for evaluating the facts of the case is the christological value of pastoral care discussed in the last chapter. The purpose of this evaluation is to discern the principle as it is contained in the facts of the case. The first part of the evaluation involves naming and discussing suffering going on in the case and caring responses to the suffering. The second part involves narrowing the focus to naming and discussing the need associated with the suffering in the case and the specific ways that the caring responses address the need. The final part of the evaluation involves discussion of the fallibility of the pastoral care in the case.

The Christological Value of Pastoral Care

It may seem unnecessary to spend time in case interpretation naming suffering and pastoral care responses to suffering because the case is about nothing other than pastoral care. However, if pastoral care is a christological value existing within the church community, finding ways to identify and name pastoral care not only is necessary but also is exceedingly important for learning pastoral care in the congregational setting. It is important for learning because pastoral care in congregations often does not occur in easily identifiable care situations. In pastoral psychotherapy, the entire conversation with a client is placed within the realm of pastoral care automatically because that specialized ministry exists as nothing else than a particular form of pastoral care. Likewise, chaplain conversations with patients also are viewed within the realm of pastoral care, though various chaplain activities are more diverse than those of pastoral psychotherapists. Pastoral care in con-gregations, however, cannot be identified so easily and clearly as one specific kind of thing done over and over that exists in separation from other aspects of ministry and church life, as the case shows. A good example comes from the congregation's response to the youth group. Some may want to view this whole situation entirely within the boundary of Christian education. But why? There is, presumably, suffering going on, and there is a caring response on the part of the church, which indicates that the value of care is playing a role in this part of congregational life, summoning the church to respond to the suffering of the youth group.

Little information is given about last year's youth group. Consequently, it is an assumption to say that there was suffering in the youth group. Taking illegal drugs and having sex at youth group events are inappropriate and potentially destructive behaviors, and these behaviors can be seen as red flags indicating that there may have been some sort of suffering related to these behaviors. For example, Robert's older sister was a member of the youth group who graduated last year. If she was one of the teens engaging in the inappropriate behavior, it becomes possible to suggest that her behavior may have been related to her relationship with her father and stepmother. Was her relationship with her parents negative as Robert's was negative? Since no information of this sort is given, the presumption of suffering in the youth group remains somewhat speculative, though the inappropriate behavior is certain.

This brings us to the response of the church to the youth group, which is where the christological value of pastoral care first can be seen. The search committee conveyed to Pastor Johnson the situation with the youth group, and in hiring her, they wanted her to lead the youth group in a more appropriate direction. Therefore, the congregation, represented by the search committee, responded to the youth group in a caring manner through the hiring of Pastor Johnson. In turn, the christological value of pastoral care can be seen in the ministry of Pastor Johnson to the youth group during the course of the nine-month period culminating in the retreat.

Identifying suffering in relation to the youth group as a whole, and the caring response to that suffering, is to some extent not very specific because it involves a group and its leadership over time. When there is not much information given, it is difficult to point toward particular instances of suffering and specific responses to it. Still, care can be seen as a value summoning the church to be concerned about the youth group and to act on that concern. Now, however, there is a twist in the plot of the story: The youth group itself becomes the part of the church manifesting the value of care, first toward Pastor Johnson and then toward one of its members, Robert, who revealed some of his suffering to the group.

The christological value of care can be seen in the group response, and particularly the response of Kim, to Pastor Johnson, who reveals personal suffering when she takes her turn in the group exercise. Pastor Johnson writes that hearing the stories about parents from the group members evoked some emotion in her, and now that she is about to share what is in her bag with the group, she feels like crying, though she does not say why. She shows the group what she has in her bag, a wooden jewelry box her father made for her. It represents her father. She tells about her father's "quiet faith" and then tells the choir story, showing how he could reach out to others and make them feel cared for, accepted, and welcomed. She also says that her bereavement following his suicide five years ago opened her eyes to the suffering of others. Her call to ministry involved her thought that she could care for others who suffer and that she would like to bring the same kinds of qualities to her ministry that she learned from her father, his quiet faith and ability to care by showing welcoming acceptance. "That was the beginning of my call, I think, and I find that I look for ways to bring what I learned from my dad with me into my ministry."

When Pastor Johnson tells about her father and her call to ministry, she begins crying. These are not tears of joy, but instead are tears of bereavement over the loss of her father. Even after five years, she cannot talk about her call to ministry without crying, because her professional identity, or her self-understanding as a pastor, is related to her father's suicide so intimately. It is not surprising for a twenty-six-year-old pastor in her first church to link personal identity and professional identity very closely, and it makes sense that some parental qualities can provide models for relating to others in ministry. For Pastor Johnson, however, talking about identity and vocation is particularly difficult because of the impact of her father's suicide.

From what is known in the case, she was twenty-one, a college student making vocational decisions in preparation for the adult world of work, when the suicide happened. Although more information would be needed for a reader to make judgments about the specific ways that the suicide impacted Pastor Johnson's life, in addition to its impact on her vocation, it does seem clear that she was affected deeply and that it has a long-term effect on her life and work. Having been through seminary, and having entered pastoral ministry, Pastor Johnson must have been required to discuss her call to ministry at certain points, and she perhaps knew from experience that she would cry when she told Kim about her call. This brings us to the caring way that Kim and the whole group respond to the pastor, manifesting the christological value of pastoral care. Kim is the only one who responds verbally, saying that she did not mean to pry and touching Pastor Johnson on the shoulder in a comforting way. Although Kim is the only one who speaks, the whole group listens.

When it comes time for Robert to tell the group what is in his bag, he confesses that he could not think of anything to put in, that he does not know who he wants to be, and that he has no one comparable to the positive role models of the other group members. Then he presents his parents as poor role models, his father neglecting him except to criticize and his stepmother being overbearing and wanting him out of the family. Robert identifies the beginning point of his family troubles as the time when his father remarried following his biological mother's death. She died when Robert was five, and his father remarried when Robert was eight. He was in grade school at that time, and now he is about to graduate from high school at age eighteen. The odd thing is that he describes the decline of his relationship with his father as though it were something recent, as if his father had remarried only two or three years ago: "You guys know that since my dad got married again he hasn't had much time for me." In reality, a decade has passed since the marriage. This is not to imply that his relationship with his father, or with his stepmother, must be better than Robert says, because there is some confirmation from the senior pastor that Robert's father has tended not to intervene between Robert and his stepmother during conflict between them. Rather, Robert's identifying his father's second marriage as the point when trouble began raises the possibility of bereavement over the loss of his biological mother being an ongoing factor in his troubled relationship with his father and with his stepmother. It is as if Robert cannot accept having a new mother and continues resenting his father for bringing her into the family and paying attention to her while not paying enough attention to Robert. More information is needed to know what family life was like during the first few years following the death of Robert's biological mother. Nevertheless, it is possible to suggest that bereavement may very well have been playing a role in the life of Robert and his family for more than a decade, even if only in the sense of causing behavior patterns between family members to go in a certain direction and become the predominant way of relating.

Telling about his parents is upsetting, and Robert begins to cry. This is when group members respond in ways that manifest the christological value of care. Jay puts his arm around Robert, and Kim, Bill, and Jane make affirming responses to him. Kim makes an astute observation, saying to Robert that he is more than he is seeing about himself from the standpoint of his parents. Then she tells him that she perceives him to be one of the nicest people she knows and that she is glad he is her friend. Next Bill chimes in, expressing appreciation that Robert stood by him during difficult periods of his life. Finally, Jane observes that Robert has never said anything mean to her during the past twelve years that they have been together in Sunday school and offers him the idea of incorporating his kindness into his identity. Later in the conversation, John seems to summarize the responses of the group members by saying that the group cares about Robert. Then he connects the group's caring with the care of God for Robert: "And if we care about you so much, then God must care about you a whole lot more." Finally, Pastor Johnson brings the group to conclusion by following up on what John said. At that point, Kim and others hug Robert.

Jesus in Solidarity with Those Who Suffer

In this part of the evaluation, the biblical image from Matthew 25, in which the kingly Jesus stands in solidarity, or unity, with those who suffer, as if they were his family, will be used. This offers the opportunity for a closer look at the suffering and caring by focusing on specific needs of the suffering and ways of addressing the needs in caring responses.

Jesus stands in solidarity with the youth group as a whole in its suffering. What need may last year's youth group have been experiencing that has possibly carried over to the present year? A clue is provided at the time of their lock-in. Pastor Johnson tells them that there can be no sex, drugs, or drinking at the lock-in or at any youth group event, or parents will be called automatically and immediately. She expresses surprise that they seemed to accept these rules without question and that they actually seemed relieved. This reaction of the youth group suggests that they were lacking boundaries for their group and that pastor Johnson addressed their need effectively when she not only set the rules for behavior but also provided a clear consequence if the rules were broken. She goes on to remark that setting the rules seemed to be the thing that established trust between her and the group and that the trust was not short-lived but instead grew during the course of the year. Because Pastor Johnson addressed the need for boundaries, the group got off to a good start and continued in a positive direction rather than reverting to last year's behavior. The stage is set for the spring retreat to be the kind of event in which it is possible for group members to care for one another. In this sense, care of the group, first through the hiring of Pastor Johnson and then through her leadership, become intertwined with care of individuals in the group.

Jesus stands in solidarity with Pastor Johnson in her suffering. In the last paragraph, Pastor Johnson is addressing the need of the youth group, but in this paragraph the group as a whole and Kim in particular are addressing her need. The pastor's suffering involves mourning in response to her father's suicide, and what she lacks is being comforted. The listening of the group, along with Kim's words and touch, address the pastor's need for comfort within the confines of the meeting under the tree. Because her bereavement and her professional identity are bound together so closely, Pastor Johnson is in the awkward position of having to reveal her grief when talking about her call to ministry. In this respect, Kim's response, "I didn't want to pry," is right on target. With the possible exception of Robert, the youth group members do not experience sharing what is in their bags as prying. To the pastor, however, sharing what is in her bag requires her to reveal something intensely personal and painful, and it becomes a real challenge for her to participate in the exercise in the same manner as the others. However, she does have the strength to risk embarrassment and rejection by allowing her grief to be revealed. This affords her the opportunity to be comforted, because the whole group is able to handle and accept her bereavement, bound as it is to her vocation, and the group is able to handle knowing that suicide was the cause of her father's death. When Kim touches her shoulder, that touch can be seen as symbolizing the group's acceptance of the pastor in the midst of her grief.

Jesus stands in solidarity with Robert in his suffering. As mentioned in the previous section, Robert's suffering seems to have three levels. The surface level is his dilemma of not having a vision of what he wants to be or a role model like the others. At the second level, his suffering involves his poor relationship with his parents. This level of suffering relates to Robert's future, present, and past. It relates to his future in the sense that the poor relationship with his parents prevents him from having a positive parental role model for envisioning an adult identity. It relates to the present in the sense that his home life is troubled and is an ongoing problem for him. It relates to the past in the sense that his difficulties with his parents have roots in bereavement over loss of his biological mother. Bereavement also can be seen as a third level of suffering in the sense that he still may be mourning the loss of his biological mother.

Robert's need, or what he lacks in relation to his suffering, can be seen in these three levels. At the first level, his suffering is expressed in terms of his need directly, which is that he lacks identity and a role model. The youth group members address this need based on their relationships with him over the years as they respond to his uncertainty about identity. They share who they experience him to be in terms of positive qualities they have experienced in him, including being a nice guy, a loyal friend, and a kind person.

Robert does not respond to them directly in terms of his uncertainty about his identity. Instead, he responds in terms of the second level of his suffering, having to do with the poor relationship with his parents. He has already indicated that he feels rejected by his parents rather than accepted and affirmed as someone who really is wanted as part of the family. And he expresses how much this hurts him. Now he tells them that Pastor Johnson's story about her father's reaching out to her friend in the choir affected him deeply: "When you talked about your dad bringing people from the outside into the center of the group, that really got to me." Then he makes the connection to the group. Just as the pastor's father made the young man feel included in the choir, so the youth group had accepted Robert and made him feel included no matter how silly he acted. The way he puts it is that the acceptance of the youth group over time is the only thing that has allowed him to feel "on the inside." This is in direct contrast to how he feels about his parents, which is unaccepted and unwelcome, never drawn from the outside to the center of the family. He is more at home in the youth group than in his family. Robert is saying that the youth group has been responding effectively over a long period to his need for acceptance, though they have not realized it.

Robert's suffering at the third level, bereavement, contains his need for comfort in the present. Although the issue of acceptance is more easily identifiable in relation to the relationship between Robert and his parents, it also can be seen in relation to his bereavement. One reason that the pastor's story about her father affected Robert so strongly may be that it was about a deceased parent who was loved and admired. In her story, the pastor implicitly conveys that her father had made her feel that her family cared for her and drew her into its center, just as her friend had experienced her father's caring for him in the choir. Consequently, at least part of her bereavement contains both the sting of losing this source of welcoming acceptance and the longing for it. Her appropriation of this fatherly quality into her own ministry can be seen as a perfectly legitimate part of her professional development and simultaneously as one way that she is working out her bereavement. It is not unreasonable to suggest that the choir story may have drawn out that part of Robert that still stings from the loss of his biological mother's welcoming acceptance and that still longs for its return. In this light, the youth group's acceptance of Robert not only during the present year but also through many years has been a sorely needed, long-term and readily available response to his need.

Yet his need has been so great that this group response could fulfill it only partially as a mitigating, or perhaps compensating, factor in his need, still leaving him in search of a role model. In this regard, Robert unwittingly tells about a surprising connection between himself and his stepmother. He describes her as militaristic, which is meant to be a very negative portrayal. She is a Nazi issuing commands, and he has to respond as if he were an obedient soldier. However, practically in the same breath, he announces to the group that he is joining the Navy, and that perhaps there he will discover his identity. Unwittingly, through the military imagery, Robert connects his relationship with his stepmother with his future vocation, in which he will search for identity. This connection between identity and vocation, related to his stepmother rather than his father, suggests that there is a further connection between bereavement, identity, and vocation. In the Navy, he will have to obey commands, perhaps reflecting a desire to obey his stepmother. Or a military vocation may reflect an attempt to become more militaristic himself and have a better relationship with her by being more like her. Either way, a more satisfactory relationship with his stepmother would be comforting. As Pastor Johnson has made clear, bereavement, identity, and vocation can be linked very closely.

The Fallibility of Pastoral Care

Just as Jesus, in Matthew 25, said to the goats that they failed to address the needs of his family and therefore his need, so those who practice pastoral care in congregations sometimes find that they fail to address the needs of those who suffer. So far, the evaluation has shown that the youth group and Pastor Johnson have responded to some pretty serious needs and have done so rather well. Among the three pastoral care situations evaluated, the main one reflecting the decline of pastoral care through neglect is the first one involving the congregation's pastoral care of the youth group during the previous year.

The fact that inappropriate behavior was going on long before the spring retreat the previous year shows that the suffering of the group was not being addressed effectively. The identity of the ordained and lay leaders that year is not stated. There was an interim associate pastor and perhaps some church members who were not back this year. These leaders failed in their care, and the congregation failed by letting the situation go unaddressed. In accord with the discussion about the atrophy of pastoral care in chapter three, there is the possibility that the postmodern influence on values, or deep symbols, was at play in the youth group. There was competition between the church and society for the values of the youth group members, the seniors in particular, and society was winning. Of course, there are extremely few "facts of the case" about the previous year, and consequently, any hypotheses about that group and their leaders should remain merely suggestive.

The postmodern critique can be turned in the direction of the adult leaders, parents, and congregation as well as toward the youth. Was the breakdown in boundaries due to the struggles of individual adults and perhaps the congregation as a whole to cope with a changing world? What was the state of the christological value of pastoral care in this congregation as a whole? How much had it declined? Admittedly, the church realized that something was not right and that the situation needed to be addressed, but they placed the youth group in the hands of a relatively inexperienced young adult right out of seminary, which put undue pressure on her. What if the retreat had gone badly for the second straight year? Possibly, this would have impacted her future at the church. Ideally, the senior pastor, the Christian Education Committee, and Pastor Johnson would have been working together in mutually supportive ways so that no one in the church was just sitting back and waiting to see what happened in the youth group. Such action would indicate that the church had a responsibility to care for Pastor Johnson through appropriate support. Churches are fallible, however. They are not perfect and should not be treated as if they were. If postmodern critique emphasizes the decline of pastoral care, it also opens up the need for care of the church and its pastors so that the church can better live out the christological value of pastoral care.

Appropriation: The Third Reading

In the final reading, I move to my own self-interpretation in light of the case evaluation in order to discover what the case has to teach me about my own pastoral care. Before doing this, however, I would like to note two additional possibilities for the third reading involving appropriation. As a case reader, I may be in an educational program or in a church group, and may be asked to participate in a group discussion for the purpose of contributing to the learning of the case author. In other words, the case author presents a case, and the group discusses it for the educational benefit of the author. In this instance, it is not my appropriation in the center of concern but that of the author, because the case author learns from case interpretation in the same way as other readers. What I contribute to the conversation should help the case author to appropriate the case meaning. For instance, in a group discussion about the case in this chapter, I would have an interest in discussing the ending of the meeting under the tree, when John said that God cares for Robert. I want to know what Robert would have said in response. The reason I want to know this is because what John said adds a whole new dimension to the issue of acceptance discussed in the evaluation. Although the case author may share this interest, she also may have a more overriding concern about how she was leading the youth group meeting and ending it. As the group leader, she had to be aware of enabling others to speak, and she had to use her judgment regarding when it was time to stop. It may be that exploring what John said would be one step toward understanding more about her group leadership at the end of the meeting. My conversation in the educational group should be in the service of the case author's appropriation.

In the second scenario, I imagine that I am a seminary student who has yet to become an ordained pastor. If being the pastor of a congregation were still in my future, what might this case say to me? Your contribution might be different, but here is my response. First, I would note that when Pastor Johnson accepted the associate pastor position, the cards were stacked against her regarding the youth group situation. Why should someone in her first full-time pastoral position have to start out with such a difficult challenge? This would serve as a word of warning to me that I should not depend on being pampered as a pastor, even in my first congregation. The second thing this case suggests to me is that even though there will be challenges, they can be met with positive results. The third thing is that I should not stereotype teenagers as people whom I view negatively. The group in this case made a remarkable comeback from the previous year, with the help of the new pastor, and they were impressive in their care of Robert. Fourth, it seems that the need for pastoral care may arise suddenly in the most unlikely of situations and that an effective response requires shifting gears quickly. Finally, reading about Robert would give me the idea that it is possible to get glimpses into family life through different means and that these glimpses can be helpful for future ministry with the family if I can use this information wisely.

Now let's see if the case can be educationally helpful to me. To do this, I must shift from giving all my attention to the case, its author, or other readers and focus on my own actual pastoral care situation seen in light of the case meaning being disclosed through interpretation. Admittedly, this shift has been happening in bits and pieces from the beginning of the first reading. Now, however, it becomes more intentional, especially because I am writing it down.

When I reflect on what this case says to me as an experienced pastor, my judgment comes into play immediately. Initially, I am choosing to focus on the part of the case meaning having to do with loss and bereavement, that of Robert and that of Pastor Johnson. I am not choosing this focus because of any loss in my own family, which would carry with it the accompanying presumption that my bereavement is affecting my ministry. Nor am I forgetting other facets of Robert's difficulty regarding his personal identity or his troubled family relations, or the larger group interaction. Instead, my judgment involves focusing on bereavement because my congregation is filled with grief, and I must encounter it and deal with it on a regular basis. This is what stands out to me, not that other things could not be mentioned. I average around six or seven funerals a year, mostly for the elderly, but not always. There are children and teenagers in my congregation who are mourning the loss of a parent.

I could focus on many facets of bereavement in my congregation, but there are two things the case meaning discloses that are very relevant for the situation in my congregation. First, the case indicates that bereavement is no respecter of time. Five years have passed since the death of Pastor Johnson's father, yet she cannot speak of his influence on her vocation without tears. Second, over the course of years, grief can remain a factor in current relationships. Robert's biological mother died when he was five, yet he still seems to be waging a battle with his stepmother, as if he has never been able to accept the loss of his biological mother. And, based on the little bit of information given about Robert's father, it appears that he has never known how to support Robert in his struggle.

When I am talking to a church member who reveals that her husband died six years ago, that normally does not have the same impact on me as if she had said that her husband died six months ago. There is quite a bit of time between six months and six years, and this passage of time tempts me to discount the possibility that bereavement is still playing an important role in her life. The case serves as a reminder for me to not discount bereavement over time but instead to realize that I am being told something that has great import for the person's present life.

This point operates on a larger scale also. Those in my congregation who grieve participate in the church community, and as pastor I experience the ways that they interact with one another and with me. I see how they relate to family members and friends. I get to know their gifts and the ways in which they contribute to the church. When tensions or disagreements arise, I see their characteristic ways of responding, and I see the ways that the congregation has learned to respond to them. It is very easy to forget that mourning may be a significant factor in the behavior of many, many church members during times of tension or disagreement. The case says to me that when I have to figure out the dynamics of a situation in my congregation, I should include bereavement as a possible factor.

If, as I lead worship on Sunday morning, I look out over the congregation and view the worshipers from the standpoint of bereavement, it can be overwhelming. This has an impact on my worship planning and preaching. For instance, some members prefer that the services always be upbeat and that I never focus on loss in any way that might cause church members to feel like crying. This issue has to do with worship and pastoral care regarding bereavement. It presents me with a kind of balancing act in which the two things to be balanced are (1) how to have worship that does not always focus on bereavement and (2) how to remain sensitive to grieving church members on a weekly basis. This issue also goes beyond worship to the overall community life of the congregation and therefore has to do with the church members as much as me.

This makes me think of Robert and what he said about the youth group: "This church, this group, this year, has been the only place I ever felt on the inside." Without ever realizing it, the congregation, the youth group, and the new pastor not only showed Robert sorely needed acceptance but gave him a place to be where he could be affirmed. As a result, he began to feel more of what was inside him, and he had a place to express it. On a larger scale, it seems to me that the congregation, its worship, its groups, its friendships should be an accepting community that gives grieving people a place to be where they can be affirmed. This, it seems to me, is a communal form of pastoral care in which those who sometimes need the welcoming acceptance of the group also become those who at other times are the ones doing the affirming.

Finally, there is no way on earth that I can escape mourning the loss of church members. Have you ever sat in your car on a side street waiting to turn left onto a busy avenue, but you have to sit there for what seems like hours? In the flow of traffic, each automobile is spaced out one car at a time just far enough apart that you can't go. Then, when one way is finally clear, you turn your head and see that the same thing is starting from the other direction. Death in an older congregation can be like this. It comes one person at a time, and just when it starts to recede into the background as a few weeks or months have passed, here comes another. Pastor Johnson's case teaches me to acknowledge my bereavement, as the pastor acknowledged hers, the difference being that hers came from a tragic loss in her family while mine comes from multiple losses in the congregation.

Conclusion

Reading the pastoral care cases of others, or applying the interpretive process to your own case, can provide a meaningful experience of learning more about pastoral care in your congregation. It can do so by helping you focus on your situation in light of the case meaning disclosed through your interpretation. The story of pastoral care told by someone else in a case may seem very different from the story of care in your congregation. However, more similarity than meets the eye may be lurking just beneath the surface, waiting to be revealed if you take the time to read, to make judgments, and to exercise your imagination.

5

What Does Pastoral Care Case Writing Do for the Writer?

This chapter addresses the question, What does pastoral care case writing do for the writer? It responds to the questions often on the minds of students, What is the purpose or value of writing about my pastoral encounters? Or, What should I expect to gain from writing about these encounters?

We believe pastoral case writing helps the writer to find his or her way about in the world of caring ministry. The philosopher Ludwig Wittgenstein once wrote, "A problem has the form: 'I don't know my way about'" (1958, no. 123). One is confused, uncertain how to proceed, unsure what steps or actions to take. We suggest that writing cases helps the writer to become better able to make his or her way about in the world of ministry. If the case is a pastoral care case, then the world of ministry is that of caring ministry.

What does it mean to say that the purpose of pastoral care case writing is to learn one's way about in the world of caring ministry? An illustration may help. Consider a preschool class of four-year-olds whose teacher is encouraging them to try writing their names. One of the girls in the class, whose name is Barbara, seems one of the most ready to embark on the task of learning to write her name.

This could turn out to be an arduous, months-long effort, or it might be accomplished in a few short weeks. In either case, relapses are likely to occur. Her teacher assumes that some progress will be made this year, but does not know how much to hope for, and has little idea whether it will take a long or short time for Barbara to "get it." The teacher writes all the children's names on a piece of paper and supplies them with paper and pencils. Barbara looks at her name, and the interest she had in the task when her teacher first proposed it begins to falter as she looks at the length of her name—seven letters long! She compares it with what the teacher wrote for the boy sitting next to her, whose name is Bob. Barbara moans, "Your name is easy, mine's hard." Bob giggles a bit and clutches his pencil. He begins marking up his paper, and his face exudes quiet confidence, even though the squiggles that constitute his name are written on three different edges of the paper, leaving the middle of the paper completely blank.

Barbara instead begins looking around the room, her eyes scanning for some other interesting activity as she prepares to bolt from the table. Her teacher notices her look of feigned boredom and quiet desperation and exclaims, "What an interesting name you have! See, there are just three letters, a *b*, an *a*, and an *r*." (It is much too early to quibble over capitals and lowercase letters.) "Once you write the first three letters, the next three are just the same." Barbara looks at her name again, and the fact that part of it repeats itself may not register with her, but her interest is rearoused, and she grabs her pencil and starts making marks. Of course, the final product bears little resemblance to the letters her teacher wrote down and challenges the claim that there are only three letters in her seven-letter name. But over the next few weeks, she makes progress. Sometimes an *a* and *r* get out of order. Other times her name doesn't stop at seven letters, but continues with a few extra *a*'s and *r*'s. Like Bob's writing, her letters go up and down the page, some finding their way into obscure corners, others standing proudly in the middle. But in time, she is able to sign her name to a piece of artwork, and when her mother sees the class's artistic efforts together on the wall, she can tell which painting is her daughter's from her signature.

What has happened here? Barbara's problem of writing her name had the form, "I don't know my way about." As her teacher began to point out some of the interesting features of her name, this seemed to requicken Barbara's indomitable spirit, and she became less daunted by the prospect of writing it. It still had its challenges. The pencil was hard to control, and the letters refused to line up or even always to look like letters. They got out of order, and once underway they didn't want to stop. But it was no longer the case that she didn't know her way about. Maybe she never really caught on to the idea that part of her name repeats itself; that might come later, at a time when she is already so adept at writing her name that the repetition of the first three letters of her name has no practical significance. Her teacher's observations, however, helped her to look at her name again and led to her picking up her pencil and making the effort. In time, her envy of Bob also subsided, and his unfair advantage actually became the basis for an invidious comparison: "My name is grand, yours is puny." Writing it still has its frustrations, its successes and relapses, but is no longer viewed as a "problem." With regard to writing her name, she knows her way about.

How did this happen? How did Barbara come to the point where she knew her way about in the world of personal name writing? Clearly, her teacher was a vital factor in this regard. Her teacher did not simply hand her a piece of paper and a pencil and say, "Barbara, write your name on this piece of paper." Nor, for that matter, did she grasp Barbara's hand and force it to make the letters perfectly the very first time. Instead, she helped Barbara get oriented to the problem and to its eventual solution. First, she wrote Barbara's name so that she could visualize it. Next, aware of Barbara's sense that the task might be too big for her, she showed her some of the features of her name that Barbara might not have noticed on her own. What Barbara saw was a long name consisting of seven separate letters. What her teacher helped her to see was that her name had a pattern to it. In effect, her teacher looked at her name analytically, and this enabled Barbara to see it more wholistically, as not just a jumble of ciphers, but as a word that had its own coherence. Thus oriented, she could view the writing of her name as something that was not an impossibility.

In a similar way, by writing a pastoral care case, the pastor-author is able to analyze the experience, and by analyzing it she finds that its larger wholeness—its gestalt—comes into view in a way she had not perceived before. The dictionary defines analysis as "a separating or breaking up of any whole into its parts so as to find out their nature, proportion, function, relationship, etc." This is the first step in pastoral care case writing. Analysis is essential.

In one sense, however, this definition may be misleading when applied to experiences in ministry, as it assumes one already knows what the "whole" itself is. While this may be the case in some fields of endeavor, in ministry the analysis will more likely lead to a better understanding of what the whole itself may be. In fact, the purpose of analysis is not merely to break an experience down into its constituent parts, as though one were only interested in dissecting things, but to enable one to gain a better picture of the whole.

For the pastor-author, this means the whole of this particular experience. This experience, however, is part of a larger whole, the pastor-author's larger ministerial world. Thus, if the pastor's goal is to become more "at home" in the world of her ministry, the experience she chooses to write about should ordinarily be one she considers representative of the whole. She *can* write about her experience of serving on an advisory board at the denominational level, but if her ministry is primarily situated in a congregation, this experience at the denominational level (while it may impress or cause envy among her pastoral colleagues) is not as representative as an experience that occurred in the life of the congregation. On the other hand, because denominational factors are a part of her larger ministerial world—and a more significant factor for her than for the majority of her congregation—they are not irrelevant to a pastoral case based on an experience in her own congregational setting.

Analysis, then, is an important key to becoming more "at home" in one's ministerial world. Of course, some ministers do not believe in analysis, perhaps because they have seen it used in a destructive manner (e.g., the weapon their fathers used to humiliate their mothers); as a so-called "rational" procedure some laity use to frustrate a pastor's hopes and dreams; or as the method the consultants use when they presume to advise the pastor on matters about which they themselves have little firsthand knowledge. There is also the widespread belief that analysis is a man's way of becoming "at home" in his world, whereas women tend to see the whole picture with its various intricacies, making analysis unnecessary or beside the point. But is this true? It might be argued that analysis per se is not a procedure at which male ministers excel over women; if anything, the reverse is true, for male ministers are more likely to engage in higher level theorizing, whereas women ministers are more likely to look at the discrete elements of a ministerial experience. How does she acquire her sense of the whole picture except by attending to its individual parts, their relationships and proportionality?

As noted in the above definition, the purpose of analysis is to better understand the proportions and relationships between the parts of the whole. Thus, the second step in the process of pastoral care case writing is understanding, that is, understanding what the problem is in a particular case. The problem of not being at home in one's ministerial world has two major parts. One is: *I* don't know my way about. The other is: The *situation* is not what I thought. When we divide the whole in this way, we see that a minister cannot be viewed in isolation, but as "a person in a situation." By analyzing the whole, breaking it down into these two elements—person and situation—the pastor-author gains insight into the relative proportions of these two grounds for not being at home in the experience. The relationship between these two elements is also illumined. In some instances, the pastor-author's own unpreparedness, naivete, insensitivity, arrogance, and so forth, bears the larger burden for the sense of not being at home in the experience. In other instances, the situation's unpredictability, deceptiveness, inchoateness, destructiveness, and so on, bears the larger burden. In the first case, the pastor-author may view the experience as a lesson to learn from. In the latter, the pastor-author may conclude that the situation would have stymied the most skilled and savvy minister imaginable: "It would have undone Jesus himself!" This, too, may be a learning experience (e.g., recognizing the need to develop the prescience to avoid such situations), but a very different kind from one that indicates the need to develop better skills.

Our illustration of a preschooler learning to write her name also enables us to see that, even as the name Barbara has a certain configuration or structure (i.e., its repetitive aspects, its employment of only three letters to make a much larger whole), so an experience in ministry has a structure that becomes apparent from the analytic process itself. As Gestalt psychologists put it, it has "formfulness," a tendency toward "pattern completion" (Peterman, 1932; Meyer, 1956). A series of musical notes may take the form of a melody, and the melody may be repeated over and over again in an anthem, thus evoking a sense of familiarity. If repeated too often, or without some variation, it may become so familiar as to be boring or tedious. Experiences that find their way into pastoral cases are likely to evoke a sense of familiarity once their formfulness becomes apparent. As it does so, the pastor-author may exclaim—in a moment of sudden recognition—"I have been here before. I should have realized that what happened last year has occurred again. Circumstantial differences kept me from seeing it until I wrote about it. I can't believe I walked into the very trap they laid for me a year ago." By recognizing the "form" of the experience, and noting its similarity to the "form" of other experiences, the pastor-author begins to see the whole configuration of the world of his or her ministry more clearly.

In short, writing a pastoral care case (according to the format set forth in chapter 2) should enable the writer to: (1) analyze a representative experience of caring ministry in order to gain a better picture of its overall form; (2) understand the personal and situational grounds for any perceived lack or absence of "at-homeness" in the experience; (3) recognize and explore similarities between this and other experiences of caring ministry; and (4) see the overall configuration of his or her ministry more clearly.[1]

The Case of a Contemporary Nicodemus

To illustrate our point that writing a pastoral care case helps the writer find his or her way about in the world of caring ministry, we will now consider a pastoral care case written by a 41-year-old Presbyterian minister. Unlike the pastoral care case discussed in chapter 4, this case was not written according to the case format presented in chapter 2, but according to a format developed for use by Doctor of Ministry students at Princeton Theological Seminary. Although this or any other format could be evaluated for its effectiveness in enabling the writer to achieve the above-stated goals, to do so in this case would divert us from our present concern to illustrate these goals.

The case involves an experience that occurred during the second year of this minister's second pastorate. He had previously served a church in the upper Midwest for seven years; during this period the congregation grew from 900 to 1400 members, and from 400 to 700 in worship attendance. In 1997, he took the position of senior minister in a northeastern city not far from New York City, explaining his move as due largely to the fact that he had grown up in the city of

---

[1] We have used the metaphor "at-homeness" in the above definition. It should be noted that "at-homeness" is not synonymous with "being comfortable," for one may (and often should) experience considerable discomfort in certain situations of ministry and yet feel at home in this discomfort, knowing that one "has been here before" and "knows one's way about" in situations of this nature. Nor do we intend this metaphor to challenge the known fact that ministers typically feel out of place in this world, both because this is the nature of the Christian calling (cf. Dittes, 1999) and for the additional reasons set forth in our discussion of postmodernism in chapter 3.

his first pastorate and had attended college there as well. He felt it would be good to experience life and ministry in a different context.

When he came to his new assignment, the congregation of 850 members was attempting to recover from the pain and conflicts of his predecessor's ministry, which had ended with allegations of sexual and financial impropriety. His initial concern was to restore peace and unity to a congregation deeply divided by the controversy, as well as by a generation gap between long-term members and an influx of newer, younger members. His long-range hope is that after unity has been restored, the congregation will be able "to connect the resources of a wealthy membership living in a residential oasis with the complex needs of the surrounding urban area." In the nearly two years of his pastorate, the church membership has grown to 900 and "much healing has taken place." His new congregation is proving more difficult to pastor than his former pastorate, however, even though it is smaller. This is partly because he does not feel truly at home there. There was a much better fit between his own theological views and those of his congregation in his former pastorate. He was also very familiar with the culture, the way people related to one another, and a host of ways of doing things that persons who grow up together take for granted.

Because his first pastorate *was* in his home town, he makes an especially good case for our discussion here, as this fact accounts for at least some of his sense of his new congregation's foreignness and his own not-at-homeness. If he had experienced his hometown as a very unpleasant place to be, a place where he was not at home, his new congregation might have felt very different. But he left his former congregation because he felt some need to leave home, apparently in order to prove himself in a setting that would be quite different from what he had known. His age–41 years old–may also indicate a "mid life transition" (Levinson et al, 1978) in which the moderate, even progressive perspective on theological issues formulated through his educational experiences and embodied in his first pastorate was suddenly subject to challenge.

The challenge did not come from members more conservative than he, but from several members (mostly from the older generation) who were more liberal, especially on matters pertaining to church doctrines. He was challenged, for example, during an adult membership class because the book of confessions (as one prospective member put it) "has stuff in there about the virgin birth, the Trinity, and the divinity of Jesus that I'm not so sure about." The pastor has always taken pride in being an enlightened person who does not believe the basic tenets of the church on blind faith or simple credulity. He has worked through these issues himself, and therefore feels that he is solidly grounded in his personal theology. This has enabled him to carry out his ministry with integrity and effectiveness. These new challenges, however, have been disconcerting, because they were very infrequent in his former congregation. He wonders if these individuals are precisely what theologians have reference to when they use language such as "post-Christian" or "postmodern." Whether this is so or not, it certainly appears to him that some members approach the church with a certain consumer mentality, deciding what aspects they are willing to "buy into," and what they will leave for other consumers.

On the other hand, he is personally attracted to these individuals, for there is something inside him that resonates with what he calls their skepticism. Thus, he finds himself in the uncomfortable position of the middleman, caught between his denomination's traditional affirmations of faith and his parishioners' apparent lack of confidence in them. In the Doctor of Ministry workshop where he presented this case, his colleagues who found themselves among more traditional believers—and who felt at home in these contexts—expressed some wonderment that these people came to church at all. He acknowledged that he sometimes wondered about this himself, yet he feels a personal sympathy with them, as he, too, is a restless seeker, having proven this in his decision not to remain in one place. Moreover, these are the persons with whom he has chosen, at least for the foreseeable future, to throw in his lot. He notes in his pastoral case that to try to understand them better, he has been reading some of the writings of Ralph Waldo Emerson, who left his own pastorate in the Unitarian Church in his early thirties, never to return to pastoral ministry. Our pastor-author perceives that "the Emersonian spirit still seems to rule local New England theology. He [Emerson] saw every created entity as a vivid reflection of the divinity that birthed it into being. He respected Jesus Christ, but drained that image of all supernature."

The case author (we will call him Brian) is known to one of us (on testimony of others) as having a fine reputation as a preacher of the gospel. While his skill as a worship leader is probably his strong suit, he attributes this not to his rhetorical skill but to his solid theological grounding, developed through careful study of the tradition and through reflection on its viability for him and others like him—intelligent, socially aware, tolerant of differences of viewpoint, and so on. He would probably describe himself as more of an educator than a preacher, and his ministry as a whole as one in which he seeks to educate (i.e., drawing his congregation out so that their lives may reflect an informed approach to the gospel and an awareness of its capacity to orient their lives).

Ideally, our presentation of the case would include the text itself. This way, readers could see for themselves how Brian went about the task of writing his case and how the writing of this case helped him find his way about in his caring ministry. Space limitations, however, require that we make substantial use of our power to play the role of editors—summarizing here, paraphrasing there, and thus, no doubt, altering his work. We can only hope that we do not distort its meaning.

Brian begins the case by stating what he believes it was essentially about. He writes:

> This [case] arises out of a pastoral encounter I had with an active member of my congregation who was, as I interpret his request, seeking a transformative spiritual relationship with God that he had not heretofore experienced. I've chosen this vignette for analysis because Bob, as I'll call him, is typical of many members of my congregation in his liberal, reason-based theology, his yearning for something more, and the difficulty he encounters with some of the Christ-centered tenets of traditional Presbyterianism...It gives me the opportunity to explore the challenges a similarly oriented pastor faces in assisting modern, secular Americans in achieving, or perhaps better, receiving, the spiritual experience they seek but don't know how to get.

In a footnote to this opening paragraph, Brian notes that the experience he is about to report "gives me the opportunity to examine how my own experiences and predispositions as a pastor both enable and prevent me from assisting parishioners to obtain that 'something more' they yearn for."

By emphasizing Bob's representativeness, Brian alerts us to the fact that he wants to use his experience with Bob to gain a clearer picture of the situation in which he finds himself. His footnote material suggests that the case additionally affords the opportunity to engage in self-examination. Because the "situational" concern appears in the body of the text, while the "personal" issue is located in a footnote, we should prepare ourselves for a pastoral case that is weighted, proportionately, toward the situational. As readers of the case, we may accept Brian's own priorities as to what he expects to learn from writing this case, or we may judge that his priorities should be questioned. That is, is the problem of not knowing his way about in his caring ministry with persons like Bob due primarily to the situation he finds himself in—a congregation of modern, secular, liberal-minded Americans—or is it due more to issues within himself that prevent him from assisting his parishioners in obtaining the "something more" for which they are yearning?

Both are important, and the fact that Brian alludes to both indicates that he understands himself to be "a person in the situation." The history of pastoral care case interpretation, however, suggests that, in general, the pastoral care case is most helpful in providing the writer assistance in personal self-examination or self-appraisal. It should also be noted that Brian has a rather wide-lens view of the situation—the congregation seen in light of modern secularism—whereas in our case format there would also be a concentrated focus on the various characters and scope of relationships. In any event, pastoral case writing seems ideally suited to learning more about why this situation causes this particular individual—*Brian*—to feel as though he doesn't know his way about in it.

Self-examination has a rich history in Christianity, dating back to Saint Augustine and continuing through nineteenth-century Methodism, and the pastoral care case may be thought of as belonging to this tradition. Unless there are compelling reasons for not doing so, priority should ordinarily be given to using the pastoral care case as an opportunity to engage in self-examination. This self-examination may, in turn, lead the writer to qualify or even question the way that he or she understood the situation. As a result of the sustained self-examination that pastoral case writing affords, the writer may see the situation—of which Bob is representative—in a new and different light. We will return to this point later in this chapter and in the following chapter as well.

Brian continues to describe the situation, noting some of the things we have already indicated about the congregation, including its geographical location, and some additional observations, such as that interfaith marriages among his parishioners are common and that "church members cobble together a supportive spiritual matrix from disparate religious sources that in former generations might have been thought of as mutually exclusive." Here, he indicates that his church members are looking to religion to provide the orientation they seek, but are not doing this in the traditional way of locating themselves in a single, coherent religious tradition.

Brian then notes another situational factor, that there are "two fairly well-defined age groups" that "dominate the congregation's demographic profile and coexist in an always amiable but sometimes uneasy coalition: the 60-somethings and the 30-somethings." Bob is among the former. Brian adds that "It would be fair to say that the typical 60-something member has led a conventionally mainline and seamless religious journey firmly rooted in 1950s American spirituality." Thus, what Brian communicates in these opening paragraphs is his interest in viewing Bob as typical of the older generation in his congregation. He uses sociocultural categories ("60-somethings," "conventionally mainline," "1950s American spirituality") in an initial effort to describe Bob's typicality or representativeness.

Brian next introduces the events leading up to his encounter with Bob. As part of a sermon series during Epiphany and Lent on the gospel of John, Brian preached a sermon about Nicodemus, who, Jesus tells him, "must be born again" (John 3:1–21). Among the "other things" he said in the sermon, he expressed the view that "although much of modern evangelical Christianity has defined the 'born-again' experience too narrowly and spectacularly for the tastes of more conventional mainline and Roman Christians who were baptized as infants and never knew an entirely godless or Jesusless day in their entire lives, that too-narrow definition doesn't preclude the importance in every Christian's life of a personally transformative religious experience or relationship with Jesus Christ." He noted that, for example, "it might be more process than event, more lifelong than once and for all, more seamless than cataclysmic, but I did say that it ought to be *there, felt,* and *real.*" This is the sum of Brian's account of the events leading up to the encounter.

Bob appears in the very next paragraph. He is described as "always one of the most careful listeners to my sermons," who, on this occasion, "was mildly but obviously troubled by what I said." Brian's next sentence involves an interpretation based on his subsequent conversation with Bob. He writes: "I think he sensed something of the truth of it (i.e., the sermon), but had no idea precisely what I was talking about or how to get it in his life." This explains why Bob did what he did: "So after the sermon he visited me in the greeting line and promised to make an appointment to talk to me about the sermon's content." We are not told what Brian may have thought at the time Bob promised to make an appointment to talk about the sermon's content. This may itself be a clue to the fact that Brian will give more emphasis to the situation than to the examination of his own reactions to Bob's request. Was he threatened by Bob's request, concerned that Bob was planning to come and criticize the sermon for being too traditional or too much like sermons preached in Baptist or Pentecostal churches? Or was he encouraged, thinking: "I get so little reaction to my sermons that it is nice when someone cares enough about what I say that they want to make an appointment to talk about it"? Brian does not say.

In the next paragraph, we learn more about Bob. He is about 60 years old, recently retired from a long middle-management career at IBM, and plans to split his retirement between his home outside New York City and a summer home in his native Maine. While in town, "he and his family are some of the most active members of the church, the kind of dream parishioners every congregation needs in order to thrive." Next we get a brief portrait of Bob, one for which Brian's earlier description of "the typical 60-something member" may have prepared us:

> Grace and dignity personified, Bob is tall, handsome, built like a defensive end, and archetypically male, although perhaps more emotionally available than many others his age in this part of the world. One of the most reliable (if not one of the most naturally gifted) basses in our church choir, he can be seen struggling valiantly to keep up with the paid bass soloist through a rolling melisma with a Latin text. You can also see that he's visibly moved by the music even as he sweats with the effort.

This is a nicely nuanced description of Bob, one that presents him in a positive light without idealizing him. Its portrayal of his contribution to the choir is observant and playful and reveals some things about the congregation that Brian's earlier, more demographic description did not disclose—that the church can afford a paid soloist and that some anthems are sung in Latin. Perhaps the most eye-catching phrase in this description, however, is that Bob is "archetypically male, although perhaps more emotionally available than many men his age in this part of the world." Thus, while his typicality is again noted, Bob's distinctiveness—his emotional availability—is also recognized, a distinctiveness that may explain why he sought a pastoral conversation with Brian, a type of encounter that many men do not seek and sometimes actively resist.

We may wonder if Brian found the men in his former location to be more emotionally available than men where he is now. If so, then Bob may have a personal significance for him that is not disclosed here, as he may be reminiscent of the men Brian knew back home. In that case, Bob's promise to make an appointment with Brian may have evoked feelings in Brian that are not disclosed in the pastoral case, such as feelings of nostalgia for what he had left behind and feelings of anticipation born of a desire for personal contacts of the kind he used to enjoy. This may, in turn, shed further light on Brian's description of Bob as a choir member, as a man who gives it all he's got, who is capable of being "visibly moved by the music." He is a man, in other words, who is capable of showing his emotions, at least where music is involved. Brian, in turn, has noticed this other Bob, though he does not say what it may mean to Brian himself.

Brian completes his portrait of Bob by mentioning his family, noting that his "lovely, kind" wife is even more engaged in the church, and that two of their four children, with families of their own, are also members. A third child is lesbian and terminated her membership over the denomination's position on lesbians and gays. Bob and his wife, while feeling betrayed by the denomination in their daughter's case, "hang in there resolutely out of long loyalty to this church." Does Brian wonder if Bob's request for a conversation about this sermon has something to do with their sense of betrayal? Or is this family material provided solely to help orient the reader to the situation?

The case continues with a few brief sentences about Bob's making an appointment a few days after the sermon, the meeting taking place in Brian's office, and the fact that Brian was not thinking at the time about his meeting with Bob as potential case material, so he is relying very much on memory "and brief notes I kept after Bob left." Although this suggests that he usually makes brief notes after most such visits, it does not say what he might have done differently were he thinking of this as a potential case. The conversation "ranged far and wide," so Brian left out the "less pertinent passages." Also, we cannot reproduce Brian's conversation material in full, but will need to be selective.

The pertinent part of the conversation begins with Bob's saying, "The other day in your sermon you talked about being born again and having a more profound relationship with God, and I wanted to know more about how to do that." Brian responds with this suggestion: "Okay, Bob, I'd love to talk with you about that, but it's a complicated subject, so maybe you could start by telling me what you heard me saying in the sermon." Bob answers that not only in this sermon, but "a lot of the time," Brian has talked about "the importance of having a personal relationship with Jesus Christ...You keep suggesting that a relationship with Jesus Christ is where the whole Christian life begins–our mission, and worship, and ethics in the world. And so I guess I'm puzzled about how to get to 'square one.' I'm not sure exactly what it is, and I'm pretty sure I've never really had it in my life before."

Brian responds by noting that most Presbyterians, including himself, are good at thinking about God, but sometimes are not "quite as good at relating to God." "Our 'growing edge' might be a more careful nurturing of that internal experience of the close presence of God in our lives." Brian's response seems exactly right to Bob, who says: "That is just what I feel I don't have and never really had in my life."

Brian requests information at this point, asking Bob to tell him something about his "spiritual journey thus far." Bob proceeds to tell about being baptized as an infant and raised in a Congregational church in Maine, about learning more in church about morality and ethics than about Jesus, and then about coming to their present location, where "the church became so important for us, as you know. It's been the center of our lives. It's where we spend most of our waking, nonworking hours, except in the summer when we're at our lake house in Maine." He indicates that the church played a vital role in helping them raise their children and continues to provide "some help for my daily life. I get moral direction." While the church "places me in the context of something larger than myself," Bob admits that "I feel close to God when we're in Maine," not because he goes to church there–he doesn't–but because he feels closer to God, as though God is "close enough to talk to" when he is among the trees and the lakes.

Brian observes that as Bob begins to talk about Maine and feeling closer to God there, his voice begins to choke and his eyes mist over. Bob continues: "Somehow when I'm by myself in the woods, I just get overwhelmed with gratitude for the undeserved beauty of the world. Then I go to watch the grandchildren swimming in the lake, and a sense of awe just takes me over. For me, that source of gratitude and awe are the essence of religion." Note here that Bob has offered his own definition of religion, one that sums up what religion means to him: gratitude, as for the undeserved beauty of the world, and awe, as when he watches his grandchildren swimming in the lake. There may, perhaps, be a question implied in this statement of his religion: Could it be that this is enough? Have I already experienced as much as religion can offer? As much as any man has a right to desire? At present, though, he feels the need for something more, and feels that Brian's sermon began to identify what this something more might be.

In his response to Bob's statement, Brian attempts to frame this experience of gratitude and awe as "a form of prayer." Bob, however, says this would apply only if "you can call prayer something without words." Then he returns to his initial question: "But what's this relationship with Jesus Christ that you keep talking about? I don't feel as if I have anything like that. I can't let myself go. My spiritual life feels all dammed up inside. I'm looking for something more, something more intimate, more enthusiasm, something. How does a person get born again? How do you get Jesus Christ to come into your heart, to use the old Sunday school language?" Brian responds with a question of his own: "Can you tell me what Jesus Christ means to you?" Bob replies that Jesus was a prophet who lived a life he could never hope to emulate, and who "knew God better than anybody in history. He does not, however, play any role at all in my life, maybe just as an example to reach up to." As indicated in Brian's earlier comments on the congregation's religious ethos, this answer seems typical of the beliefs of its "60-somethings." It does not ascribe divinity to Jesus, nor give much credence to the doctrine of the Trinity.

Brian invokes the Presbyterian affirmations of faith at this point: "Members of Presbyterian congregations are asked to confess Jesus Christ as Lord and Savior. What do these titles 'Lord' and 'Savior' mean to you?" Bob answers: "I'm not sure they mean much of anything at all." "Well, then, would you say that he's a living presence in your life?" "No, 'living' is where I get stuck. I guess I'd say that his memory inspires the church's life, and his example guides our conduct. But I don't think he's alive or anything." This seems to indicate that the resurrection is also not a part of his belief system, and Brian perceives this: "Do you believe in a *risen* Christ?" "No. Maybe I believe it is a metaphor for his living memory and example. I believe that the Church is his ongoing presence in the world. But he's not personally alive or anything." "Do you believe in life after death?" "No, this life is it. But that's okay. It's enough. It's so beautiful that it's enough. I don't need the crutch of the doctrine of life after death." Thus, if Bob is seeking something more, it is not assurance of a personal resurrection, but a sense or feeling of rebirth reflected in some form of emotional release.

How Brian felt about this series of queries and responses is not indicated in the case itself. Later, in his commentary on the conversation, however, he discusses "the problematic of the church's Christ-centered confession and the place of the Christ-skeptical within the church." He describes Bob as typical of his generation. They are persons who "don't know what to do with Jesus. Their honorable, often sacrificial lives seem shaped by his risen presence, but theologically, Jesus is sometimes the poor stepchild of their spiritual matrix, especially in that hideous business on the cross and that intellectually implausible business of the resurrection. Since sin and guilt play no practical role in their thinking, the reconciling death of Jesus on the cross becomes a curiosity. Since life on earth seems to be enough for them, they hope for little more after death." This creates certain problems for Brian, for "Whenever I talk about eschatology and resurrection in anything more than the blandest metaphorical language, their eyes glaze over with the irrelevance of it, or go wide in unbelief." Although Brian may be indulging in a bit of hyperbole here, his diagnosis of the problem is significant: "I get the feeling that in their formative years they didn't hear much about this stuff." Bob's own testimony seems to confirm Brian's point, as he indicates that he was not introduced to these ideas when he was growing up in Maine (though he does allude to Sunday school language about getting Jesus to come into one's heart).

In his commentary, Brian wonders aloud whether Bob, a native New Englander, is a sort of Emersonian. In the days and weeks after their conversation, Brian "kept wondering where I'd encountered Bob's nature-centered awe before, and then I finally figured it out." It was his own earlier exposure in college to Emerson, with whom he now decided to reacquaint himself. His quotation from Emerson's address to the senior Divinity class in Cambridge (later Harvard Divinity School) is especially appropriate to this pastoral case, as it concerns Emerson's comment about preachers: "I once heard a preacher who sorely tempted me to say I would go to church no more. Men go, thought I, where they are wont to go, else no soul entered the temple in the afternoon. A snow storm was falling around us. The snow storm was real; the preacher was spectral; and the eye felt the sad contrast, in looking at him, and then out of the window behind him, into the beautiful meteor of the snow" (Emerson, 1983,

81). In Brian's view, "In Bob's experience too, the snow is more real than the bloodless discourse."

Their conversation continues, however, with Bob asking Brian point-blank whether he himself has had "this born-again experience." Brian responds that it may be more accurate to say he is "being born again," in the "sense that rebirth is a lifelong process." As for what makes Jesus a "living presence" in his life, Brian says, "I feel his pull, or his touch, or something, sort of a gentle persuasion to justice and truth and honor, a constraint of the less attractive parts of my character." "Then does he speak to you?" "No." "Then does he get his point across in some nonverbal way, (such as) a clear intuition in your mind of something, or a clarity in decision making that you feel comes from him, or something like that?" "Not often very clearly. I can't say we have conversations, even of the nonverbal kind. I can't say he ever gives me the kind of clarity I'd be more comfortable with. But somehow deep down in my brain or heart, he gets his point across."

The conversation continues in this vein a bit longer, with Bob repeating his earlier statement that "I don't know how to get that. I don't know how to let myself go. I don't know how to release whatever it is that's dammed up inside of me." Brian suggests that he try an experiment in which he prays "as articulate a prayer as you can in the name of Jesus," trying "to ask God as specifically as you can for what it is you feel you're missing in your life." Bob responds that, though he is not very good at prayer or silence, he is willing to give it a try. Their conversation closes with Brian's suggesting that Bob also do some reading "on how other bright skeptics have come to an encounter with Jesus." When Bob says that he would "love to," Brian proposes that he read "three brief and accessible accounts of spiritual experience by faithful skeptics, or doubting believers." Brian suggests Frederick Buechner's *The Sacred Journey* (San Francisco: Harper & Row, 1982); Marcus Borg's *Meeting Jesus Again for the First Time* (San Francisco: Harper San Francisco, 1994); and Anne LaMott's *Traveling Mercies* (New York: Pantheon, 1999).

What clearly stands out in Brian's account of his conversation with Bob is its focus on experiencing Jesus in a very personal way. Especially noteworthy in this regard is the way they query each other about their views and experiences of Jesus. Brian's questions focus more on what Bob believes about Jesus ("What do these titles 'Lord' and 'Savior' mean to you?" "Do you believe in the *risen*

Christ?"), while Bob's emphasize how and in what ways Brian experiences Jesus ("Does he speak to you?" "Does he get his point across in some way?" "Is he a clear intuition in your mind or something?"). Brian's questions mainly elicit responses from Bob that there are serious deficiencies in his experience of Jesus, whereas Bob's questions elicit responses that lead him to exclaim, "I don't know how to get that."

Conceivably, Bob is engaging in some idealization of Brian, assuming that Brian's responses reveal personal experiences that Bob can only imagine. At any rate, once the conversation shifts from belief *about* Jesus to experience *of* him, it takes a more self-disclosing direction, similar to Bob's account of his solitary walks in the woods and his overwhelming sense of gratitude for the "undeserved beauty of the world." Had it continued in this vein, it might have led to a shared recognition that their experiences of Jesus—and desires for an even more personal experience—were not very different. They might have sensed that they shared a common problem, the desire for more of what they had both experienced rather vaguely and episodically. They may even have struggled to find some way to find their way about in this problem together. For example, they might have followed Bob's hunch that it has something to do with being "dammed up inside." Is Brian's pastoral care case itself symptomatic of an emotional logjam? And is this why he gave greater priority to the situation than to his own self-processing? We will explore these questions in more depth in the next chapter.

Brian reports that when Bob returned for a second visit one month later, he had not been "diligent in the disciplines I suggested." Also, Brian says that he "got the feeling" this time "that in the first meeting [Bob] had come not only to find out how to receive a spiritual experience but to check out the acceptability of the faith he then held." In his further remarks on the first visit, Brian confesses that he is not at all sure how a pastor can help a parishioner achieve or receive something that "seems to come to us as a gift." He observes that he has "a vague idea of the kind of thing" Bob is after, but that he himself "has not been beneficiary to the kind of added dimension of emotion that Bob seems to be seeking," and thus seems "of minimal use as a spiritual adviser to Bob in this matter." This confession, which comes at the end of his pastoral care case, is especially noteworthy, because it points to the fact that Brian experiences himself in such conversations as "not at home" and as not really knowing his way about in conversations of this kind. Ironically, it is not Bob the skeptic who creates this feeling or perception in Brian but Bob the seeker, who is after something more liberating, emotionally speaking. Here, at the very conclusion of the case, Brian *does* engage in self-examination, shifting from analysis of the situation to self-analysis. Without sustained self-analysis comparable to his situational analysis, however, the "whole" of what happened between himself and Bob remains elusive.

As a result, his analysis of the situation itself—as represented by Bob—may also be somewhat inaccurate. As noted earlier, his professional colleagues had little difficulty with his depiction of Bob as a skeptic. In fact, to many of them, Bob was simply an unbeliever. Although Bob's views on fundamental Christian doctrines certainly qualify as skepticism, the reader who is attentive to the deeper level of the conversation would find grounds for challenging this rather facile depiction of Bob as a skeptic. He is much more than this. This may, in turn, raise questions as to whether Brian's general characterization of the "60- something" members of his congregation as having a "reason-based theology" is entirely accurate. Bob's comments about his gratitude for the undeserved beauty of the world, if at all typical of these older members, challenges this view of them. In fact, it could be argued that it was Brian, not Bob, who exhibited a more "reason-based" demeanor and perspective during their conversation.

Significantly, Brian's pastoral colleagues who had had a "born-again experience" along the more evangelical lines mentioned in his sermon questioned his motives for preaching a sermon on an experience he could not claim as his own. They proceeded to explain how he might have responded more effectively to Bob's questions about being "born again." Some thought Brian had missed a wonderful opportunity to help Bob have such an experience, and they wondered if such an opportunity would ever present itself again. They challenged Brian's claim that Bob had actually come to check out the acceptability of the faith he already held and argued that, because of Brian's ineffectiveness as a spiritual counselor, Bob's desire to be "reborn" dissipated between the first and second conversation.

Another way to look at it, however, is that the heart of the problem was not Brian's failure to communicate to Bob how he could have a "born-again experience," but the fact that he did not know his way about in a conversation that required him to be available to his own emotional depths. We might note in this connection that, whereas *Bob* did not fulfill his reading assignments, the encounter prompted *Brian* to go back to an author, Ralph Waldo Emerson, to whom he had been introduced in college. His reading of Emerson's address and his specific reference to Emerson's comment that preachers seem locked into "bloodless discourse" could be an indication that Brian is undergoing some internal changes. These may be reflected in his effort to preach on subjects he had not felt a need to preach on before. Could it be that these sermons are reflective of some deep, if unexpressed, desire to overcome his own sense of being emotionally dammed up inside? If so, the problem that is central to this pastoral case—what the case is most truly about—is the writer's need to find his way about in his own internal world. This means, in effect, that Brian is as much the Nicodemus in the story as Bob appears to be.

Conclusion

We have suggested in this chapter that pastoral care case writing helps the author to find his or her way about in the world of caring ministry. Put another way, it helps the author become more "at home" in this world, especially by coming to a better understanding of the situation, on the one hand, and of one's self—the *person* in the situation—on the other. By examining this case of a modern Nicodemus, we have noted that gaining a better understanding of self is likely to lead to a reappraisal of one's initial understanding of the situation as well. However, this case also draws our attention to the fact that self-analysis is likely to be more difficult than analysis of the situation. This may be due to defensiveness (as is sometimes alleged by readers of pastoral care cases), but it may also be due to the fact that one is simply less skilled in self-analysis, having received less training in how to do it.

This raises the question with which the next chapter is concerned, namely, whether there might be something inherent in the pastoral case writing itself that biases the process more toward situational analysis than self-analysis. That is, does pastoral case writing, for whatever reasons, limit the degree to which one is able to engage in self-examination? If this were the case, it would not invalidate the pastoral care case as a learning method or tool, but it should at least encourage us to supplement pastoral case writing with other methods that are also designed to help pastors become more at home with themselves in the world of caring ministry.

6

The Limitations of the Pastoral Care Case

In this chapter, we will consider the limitations of the pastoral care case. By noting its limitations, we can begin to address the question of whether the limitations are inherent in the genre or primarily due to its traditional uses (i.e., in educational contexts). This could lead, in turn, to the creation of other forms of writing to supplement case writing.[1]

In noting the limitations of the pastoral care case, we will not emphasize the point made, for example, by Charles V. Gerkin in *Widening the Horizons* (1986), that the pastoral case model's horizons should be widened by taking into consideration the community where the congregation is situated. Although Gerkin makes an important point, and presents a compelling case that illustrates the interactive influences of church and community (1986, chap. 4), we believe that this addresses the situational dimension of a pastoral

---

[1] In this chapter, we use the term *pastoral care case* as advocated in chapters 2–5. In noting the limitations of the pastoral care case here, we do not single our model out for special critique, as we have perceived this limitation in cases written according to all case formats with which we are familiar. Instead, we are pointing to a limitation of pastoral case writing, one that defies easy explanation and solution.

care case—expanding it, as it were—but does not address the limitation that concerns us here, as foreshadowed in the previous chapter.

There are also those who have argued that pastoral care cases often lack a "theological dimension." While this allegation has some merit, the case formats with which we are familiar include the instruction to reflect theologically on the pastoral experience. It is perhaps more accurate, therefore, to say that writers of pastoral care cases have found this requirement to be an especially difficult one to meet, and we have therefore offered assistance in this regard in chapter 3. The reasons for this difficulty are certainly complex, but the onus should not be placed on those who require seminary students to write pastoral care cases. In fact, they are usually the ones who find themselves in the position of cajoling students to give more attention to the theological aspects of their cases, for this, it would appear, does not come very naturally to the novice writer of a pastoral care case.

Rather, we are concerned here with an even more fundamental limitation. It has much to do with the fact that the pastoral care case is an educational text. Being an educational text, it is usually written with other readers in mind. The fact that the author is aware that it will be read by others necessarily influences what gets included in—and excluded from—the text. Many forms of religious writing are not written for others to read, including spiritual journals, letters addressed to God, private poems, anonymous notes affixed to religious objects (such as crosses and statues), and so forth. Sometimes the author has another reader in mind, such as a spiritual director or very close friend, and, when this is the case, it is likely to influence what gets written, however imperceptibly. The pastoral care case, however, is at several removes from such private forms of writing. When it is used in an educational setting, there is the anticipation that several individuals will read it. This is an integral part of the educational process, for the more perspectives that are brought upon the case, the more potential there is for its being a rich and valuable learning experience not only for the author but also for the readers.

On the other hand, very little attention has been given to the question of what is left out of a case by virtue of its educational nature. Much, of course, is said about protecting the confidentiality of the parishioner. The attention given to this matter, however, obscures the fact that much more gets "written out" of a case than the name of the parishioner. In our view, the aspects of the experience that most systematically get written out are the underlying psychological elements involved. Thus, unlike those who say that the pastoral care case is too psychological (meaning not theological enough), we argue that it is likely to be not psychological enough, and perhaps cannot be, because of its public nature. Although we do not wish to challenge the argument that the pastoral care case is susceptible to a dearth of theological content, we question the implication that for it to be more theological, it must be less psychological. On the contrary, if its psychological dimension could be deepened, its theological dimension would be strengthened and deepened as well.

The Emphasis on Social Roles

What do we mean by our claim that the underlying psychological elements of the experiences are characteristically written out of a pastoral care case? Our answer lies, in part, in the fact that a pastoral care case is ordinarily about relationships a pastor has with one or more parishioners. We have noted in chapter 2 some of the ways in which this relationship differs from what occurs in pastoral psychotherapy: that it precedes the encounter presented in the case; that it is complex because pastor and parishioner relate to each other in other settings where their roles are different, sometimes reversed; and that the pastor is likely to have a relationship with other members of the parishioner's family. These are important differences, and they have important effects on the case itself. The very multi-dimensional nature of the pastor-parishioner relationship makes the pastoral care case potentially more complex than the pastoral psychotherapeutic case.

On the other hand, experience indicates that it also has a limiting effect. The very fact that the pastor has more than one relationship with the other person makes it more likely that their relationship will be presented in largely social terms (i.e., roles). For example, Brian introduces Bob in this way: "Grace and dignity personified, Bob is tall, handsome, built like a defensive end, and archetypically male, although perhaps more emotionally available than many other men his age in this part of the world." This is a nicely balanced portrayal of Bob, but instead of following up on what it means to Brian to say that Bob is "more emotionally available," his description continues with a comment on Bob's reliable participation in the church choir. It is not that Bob is being defined by his role as a choir member, but the relevance of this feature about him leads to the tendency of a pastoral care case to move toward the psychological surface. We are more than our social roles, yet pastoral care cases tend to identify the persons involved by these roles, whether these are roles in the community or in the congregation itself.

To illustrate the point further, here are the introductions provided for several parishioners who were the focus of cases written by a group of highly experienced pastors:

- "The story begins with a call to my office for an appointment from a young woman who is a very active member of Second Presbyterian Church."
- "The major participant in the experience is Shirley, a retired nurse in her late sixties."
- "Brandi is a college junior and director of the Christmas program. In my opinion, she is a wonderful young woman, who is very committed to her church, but is kind of a 'Lone Ranger.'"
- "The following report is based on a verbatim reconstruction of my brief e-mail correspondence with a middle-aged, single, female parishioner."
- "Linda is a lifetime member of the congregation. She is in her mid-30s. She is the daughter of parents who have a direct connection to the founding of the church."
- "Julie, in her late thirties, is the daughter of an 'old' church family. Both of her parents are living and are active participants in the life of the congregation. Her father, prior to retirement, was a successful local businessman; her mother is actively engaged in the local social scene, particularly a garden club."

Compared with these rather general, nondescript introductions to the major participant in the cases, Brian's portrait of Bob tells the reader much more about how Brian views Bob personally, and how Bob affects Brian personally. Still, his description also moves quickly into an effort to "place" Bob in the role he plays in the church, followed by a description of Bob's family. This opening sentence from another experienced pastor's pastoral care case is refreshingly different: "If I feel a need to talk to someone about Faith Church, it is often Charlotte." This single sentence communicates that Charlotte is personally important to the writer for reasons other than that she is active or related to a long-standing member. We may learn more about Charlotte in this sentence—even though she is not identified by age, occupation, and so on—than from the more detailed, but largely sociological introductions in the cases cited above. Why? Because the writer has alluded to *his* need to talk to *her*. He enters the world of caring ministry via *his* need, not *hers*, and yet, as the case develops, the conversation proves helpful to her, not least in regard to her need to be needed.

It may be objected that these introductions are merely preliminary and that the case presents the parishioner in a more personal light as it moves into the specifics of the case. For the most part, however, this is not true of the cases noted above. The personal meaning the parishioner has for the pastor and the emotions evoked in the pastor are rarely disclosed, even considered important, either for the writer to reflect on or for the reader to understand. Even the case of Bob, which is somewhat more revealing of the pastor's feelings toward the parishioner, is considered significant by its pastor-author because Bob represents a class of people, the "60-something" members whose religious spirituality was shaped in the 1950s. Had Bob read this pastoral care case, he might have felt that such efforts to categorize him were somewhat patronizing. What if the tables were turned, and he presented Brian as a 40-something, Baby Boomer preacher whose religious spirituality was shaped by the Reagan era? Would Brian have protested that his unique individuality, his personhood, had been overlooked? Could it be that Bob's problem—the sense of feeling "dammed up inside"—is due, in part, to the very fact that he *is* treated by the pastor and other members of the congregation as representative of all the other persons he superficially resembles?

The Absence of Introspection

This tendency of the pastoral care case to portray individuals in social-stereotypical ways leads into our primary point that even as parishioners are portrayed in stereotypical ways, so the authors of cases tend not to see the writing of a case as an opportunity to engage in serious and sustained introspection of themselves. That is, they present *themselves* in equally social-stereotypical ways. The dictionary defines introspection as "a looking into one's own mind, feelings, reactions, etc.; observation and analysis of oneself." We suggest that this is often missing from pastoral case writing.

The case format that Brian used does include a section called "self-critical appraisal." This, however, normally elicits a paragraph or two in which the author indicates how she might have performed or functioned better. One "self-critical appraisal" written by an experienced pastor begins this way: "Clearly, a basic task during this ministry experience was the modeling of a discernment-based methodology. Equally clear to me, I abandoned that model for a more institutional, authoritarian role when challenged." Here is another "self-critical appraisal" in a pastoral case involving the pastor's desire to develop a ministry of spiritual-direction:

> In addition to the reflective comments that have already offered some critique regarding my ministry performance, two further issues deserve mention at this opportunity. The first is an observation regarding the way in which my primary question opened a line of inquiry that was not at first perceptible. In beginning my analysis with a discussion of the appropriate technique or procedure involved in the process of spiritual direction, I found myself continuing to push beyond such methodological concerns in search of something of an entirely different order. The real issue now seems to be not so much an identification of process dynamics, but a description of the qualities of authentic personhood and spiritual process that pertain to such a process.

Methodology, model, role, performance, description—these are the sorts of preoccupations that inhibit a deeper, more introspective view of oneself as pastor. There is some irony in the fact that these terms prevail in a pastoral case involving the pastor's efforts to provide spiritual direction for his parishioners.

Of course, excerpting these statements from a case is not entirely fair, as they have meaning only within the context in which they were written. Yet our point is that the instruction to engage in "self-critical appraisal" elicits responses of this nature, and seems not to encourage a more introspective form of written discourse. To be sure, Brian's self-critical appraisal has a more self-conscious feel to it. It begins: "As a pastor, I felt myself to be both singularly qualified and profoundly ill-equipped to help Bob: singularly qualified because there's enough Emersonianism and modernist skepticism in me to provide me with the grace to understand and sympathize with his struggles, and profoundly ill-equipped because I haven't heard Jesus speaking to me in the way Bob, it appears, thinks should happen." Even this observation, however, fails to reflect the introspective process to be described later. Because it fails in this regard, it also seems to misinterpret Bob. On the one hand, it overemphasizes the "skepticism" that Bob exhibits. On the other, it ascribes to him a desire he does not seem to express, that is, to hear Jesus actually speaking to him, as though he seeks an auditory hallucination. The questions Bob puts to Brian indicate that he has something much more subtle in mind.

Before embarking on a more detailed discussion of introspection, however, we need to make very clear that we are not judging the individual pastors from whose cases we have quoted here. Their "self-critical appraisals" are generally accurate self-assessments of their strengths and of areas of possible growth and improvement. Rather, we are concerned that pastoral case writing itself does not favor an introspective kind of writing. Whether a change in its format or design (such as those we have set forth in earlier chapters) would help in this regard is an open question. But there are grounds for not being very optimistic about this. An important reason for this is that pastoral care cases are designed to be read (and interpreted) by others, and are therefore self-disclosing. We believe that the requirements of self-disclosure often, perhaps typically, produce a reluctance to engage in self-examination. That is, self-disclosure and self-examination often work at cross-purposes. It may also be the case that the very requirement to be self-disclosing—and the emphasis given to this in group processes—assumes that one knows how to engage in self-examination, an assumption that is typically untrue. The ability to engage in self-examination should not be assumed. It is a skill that can be learned; yet, in general, in the contexts in which pastoral care cases are used for pedagogical purposes, self-examination is rarely taught.

Of course, even the question of how self-disclosing a pastoral care case can be is itself an issue. If, for example, sexual misconduct among clergy is the widespread problem it is said to be, why are there few pastoral care cases in which the minister who engaged in sexual misconduct writes about it? To write a pastoral care case involving the writer's own sexual misconduct is not, in principle, an outlandish suggestion, for there are ministers who represent their sexual attention to a parishioner as being "pastoral" in nature (Graham, 1992, 228). In addition, such a case could have enormous educational value. But, assuming that any pastoral care case involves some degree of self-disclosure, we believe that this tends to inhibit the deeper self-examination that the pastoral care case is often said—or assumed—to promote.

Also, because the author is ordinarily free to choose what experiences to write about, we should not be surprised if the experiences reflect a narrow slice of the author's ministry. Many of the more troubling or humbling experiences in our professional lives are ones we prefer to forget. If so, how realistic is it to expect that these experiences will appear in cases when the author knows they will be discussed by other students or colleagues? If there is already considerable mistrust among pastors because of such issues as competition for the more desirable congregations, being on opposing sides of highly divisive theological and political matters, and so on, why expect that pastors will use the pastoral care case to explore their most troubling thoughts about their ministries? And yet those situations and experiences that go to the very heart of one's despair are precisely the ones that have the greatest educational potential. Thus, the vast preponderance of cases are ones in which the pastor is rather securely in her "role" of preacher, teacher, counselor, administrator, and so forth, and are ones that center on the pastor's "performance." If difficulties or problems are presented in the case, they usually involve momentary lapses ("I fell into the authoritarian role I was determined to avoid"), correctable misjudgments ("Next time, I won't let the budget committee sandbag me"), or other similar reasons for believing that, although the author did not "perform" as "effectively" as he might have, no great damage was done, and next time will probably go better. Such modest forms of "self-critical appraisal" are not to be disparaged, especially since the fate of one's ministry may turn on precisely these kinds of lapses and their avoidance. They may tell us very little, though, about what is most deeply troubling to the pastor-author about his or her ministry.

These comments should not be misunderstood as advocacy of a "let it all hang out" approach to self-disclosure. The point, rather, is that the requirement of self-disclosure has two main, unintended effects: It leads to the decision to choose episodes that suggest the writer is in rather good control of the situation, and it leads to a reluctance or inability to engage in penetrating self-analysis, that is, in serious and sustained introspection. What, then, is introspection?

What Is Introspection?

Our discussion begins with an example of introspection from Carl Goldberg's *Understanding Shame* (1991). While this illustration is also self-disclosing, the feature of it that primarily interests us is the way in which he engages, seriously and systematically, in a process of introspection. Goldberg is a psychoanalyst in private practice in New York City. His introspections were evoked by an extremely troubling session with a client he had been seeing for about a year. He reports on this case in a chapter titled "The Shameful Secret," which bears the epigraph, "Nothing is so oppressive as a secret." His account begins this way:

> The early winter rain descended upon my consulting room with a rhapsodic resounding. At the same time, the intense resentment I was experiencing toward Vincent, my analysand lying on the analytic couch, was more than a match for the cascades of rain. My fitful mood was alarming to me. The prolonged downpour had been predictable. The weather reports had forecast that we would be bound by several days of showers. My inner displeasure with Vincent, on the other hand, was unexpected, unsettling, and unfathomable. I was a psychoanalyst, then beginning my career. I was well trained and clinically experienced. Yet I realized with concern that wintry day with Vincent that I was barely managing to keep my resentment to myself. Because of a strong, unusual reaction to a patient, I assume that my patient and I share a secret. Our mutual concealment may lie at the heart of my understanding him. (163)

This paragraph is followed by a second one that states, "I will start at the beginning. Something curious was happening in Vincent's session that morning. But I was not aware of how remarkable this session would prove to be until moments before the analytic hour was to end" (163–64). What Vincent revealed during this hour was the fact that he held himself responsible for his infant son's death. This revelation did not come all at once, but in stages, beginning with some observations about how his father had kept his emotions private, cloaking his sadness with merriment and good cheer. Then he began to talk about his own cowardice. During this phase of the session, Goldberg notes that he was

> aware that the room in which we were meeting had become less comfortable than before Vincent's session started. Unexplainably, his clothes looked more threadbare than usual. I wondered if it was the lighting in the room. It seemed darker than I remembered it. I was not even certain what the colors in the room were. The various hues were verging

into a somber gray. My attention to the depressing climate in the room alerted me to some danger imminent, but yet unspoken. Some vulnerable part of my psyche was keeping me from following my intuitions. I was still not aware of why I was fearful. (168)

He returned his attention to Vincent for further clues and realized that unlike earlier sessions, when Vincent would desperately seek his approval, asking Goldberg to comment on what he had been saying as a means to gain reassurance, this time things were different:

His not trying to draw me into his monologue was at odds with his usual style of relating with me. It seemed this morning he needed my presence, but, at the same time, required that I not enter into his narrative. The position I felt I was being placed in had an alarming knell. He was relating to me like a guilty parishioner to his priest to hear a shameful secret that he was compelled to confess. As a priest, the listener was being required to participate ritualistically, but without personal feelings or subjective judgment. (168)

Sensing his exclusion from Vincent's monologue, Goldberg finally asked him if he had any awareness of Goldberg's presence. Vincent turned in his direction for the first time, and spoke as if from a disturbing dream, saying, "It is odd that I, who have known all the vanities of the world, am asked this question!" (169). Goldberg found this a rather strange response until he recalled that it was taken from an Italian opera, *Don Carlos*, which he luckily knew a little about. He asked Vincent to refresh his memory on what the story of *Don Carlos* was about, and Vincent replied: "It is about a mad king, who kills his son and is condemned to live forever as his own son might have lived. But since he had never given himself the opportunity to know his son, he finds the requirement impossible. He is unable to find out who he, himself, is and might have become" (170).

Goldberg noted that in the year Vincent had been in therapy he had not mentioned having had any children. In fact, during the psychological history intake in their first few sessions together, he had made no mention of marriage. Goldberg looked outside the window, "as if I expected to find the mystery of how his son died in the muddy field below my window. It had been raining heavily for the past three days. The mud had formed deep funnels of water, giving the impression of canals of wet clay" (171). He recognized this surge of emotion in himself as resentment, largely because he had been kept completely in the dark for a whole year about this aspect of Vincent's life. He was able to control his expression of feeling only by repeating to himself some basic principles of psychological interviewing: "'Tell me about your son and what happened to him,' I said, hearing my voice as it may have sounded in my first year of clinical training" (171). Vincent responded with a lack of emotion that, for Goldberg, "was harrowing":

> I think I killed him. I never found out how he actually died. I was afraid to really know. He was just an infant. My wife was away from the house on an errand. I was trying to meet a deadline on a news story. The writing was not going very well. He kept crying. I raised my voice, shouting at him to shut up. He was too young to understand. I immediately realized that yelling at him would only make things worse. I went over to his crib and just tried to reassure him. Soon he became quiet. But he stared at me like he felt abandoned by me. After I went back to my desk I soon forgot about him. The story I was working on started to fall into place. When my wife came home, she looked in on him. Then, I heard the most anguished scream I've ever experienced. Nothing I've ever heard in war sounded so indignant...I went over to her and looked at the child. I instantly knew that he was not breathing. I also realized that I must have killed him. But I didn't know how or why. But, then, it would not have mattered whether or not I had intended it. My son's death was like a horrible nightmare. It was the inevitable unfolding of my fate. (171–72)

Vincent went on to relate how he had been able to keep his depression from overwhelming him until that moment. But when his son died, it was obvious to him that his ability to feel adequate and good about himself would always elude him: He observed how his fate long before his birth had destined that he would never have a confidant and friend, and he noted that his father never spoke to him of his sister's death or the other unfortunate griefs in his life: "I have come to suspect that he caused his sister's death by somehow trying to break up her affair... I became ashamed of a man I had always so highly admired. What I had regarded as his dashing ways I realized was really cowardice. I was never the son he wanted. I, too, have been denied a son with whom I can share the painful entrails of my life. There will never be anyone to understand me, or anyone who even would care to try!" (172).

As Vincent's story unfolded, Goldberg was aware of his own agitation toward him. Intellectually, he recognized that this disturbed man was revealing his painful suffering and that his own task was not to determine what really happened to his son or, least of all, to adjudge guilt. Nevertheless, Goldberg kept focusing on Vincent's bland and controlled manner, especially his lack of compassion for his child. Why was Goldberg being so critical of Vincent? He had treated vicious criminals before. Several of them had brutally raped and murdered: "I did not admire or respect them, but I did not regard them with the intense resentment I felt toward Vincent at that moment" (172–73). Then a second thought began to "intrude" on him:

> It seemed to feed on my need to justify my resentment. I felt unwilling to let go of the realization that Vincent had largely ignored and excluded me during the session. It was unlike me to be so egocentric in a therapeutic session. Yet I self-righteously reviewed in flashbacks the many occasions that I had made myself available to give Vincent a session within a few hours of request, at considerable inconvenience, when he incurred some particular stressful event. (173)

During the last few minutes of the session Goldberg sat in self-contained silence, afraid to speak, lest his unreasonable resentment erupt. He knew that if he permitted this to happen, it would embarrass him, harm Vincent's precarious self-esteem, and irretrievably contaminate their working relationship. Because the intense resentment he was experiencing toward Vincent was not his usual feeling toward Vincent, he assumed that his own unresolved conflicts were somehow involved (173).

The next morning, Vincent called Goldberg's answering service and left a message that he would not be coming for his scheduled appointment. This was the first time he had canceled an appointment. Although Goldberg was concerned about the reasons for his cancellation, he "was more relieved in not having to see him" (174). He spent Vincent's analytic hour "sitting alone in my consulting room, looking again out into the mud. The rain finally stopped. The tranquility of the morning after the rain served me with an awareness that the mud below had special meaning for me. I found out why a few minutes later" (174). He sat at his desk, and a poem he had written a year ago began to come to mind. He had written the poem the day of his father's funeral the year before. Apparently, some communication Vincent had conveyed about the death of his son and the loss of hope of their companionship had joined in Goldberg's own psyche with the resentment he had always harbored toward his own father for not giving him understanding and, thereby, not accepting who he was. His father, similar to Vincent's father, left him with the feeling that he was inadequate and couldn't take proper care of himself: "The resentment I felt toward Vincent, I assumed with shameful realization, was being shaped by the animosity I held toward my father for his viewing of me as a person who will not leave his mark on the world. Vincent's excluding me in the session had reopened a psychic wound for me" (175).

The next several pages of Goldberg's chapter give an account of his relationship to his own father and involve a discussion of "aspects of my life that analysts rarely, if ever, reveal. Not to speak of these events would make it difficult to understand why Vincent had such a disturbing effect on me" (176). We will not include this account here, but only note that in his "session with myself" in Vincent's absence, Goldberg became "aware that I had not finished my work with my psychological father. Vincent's ostensibly emotionless description of his son's death had brought back disturbing aspects of my relationship with my father that, apparently, I had not sufficiently worked through and resolved" (178). Also, Vincent's strange use of the word "indignant" to describe his wife's reaction to their son's death provided "a key clue to my side of the shared mystery with Vincent...Was my father indignant and resentful that I hadn't permitted myself to recognize him as the lonely and hurt person he was? Shamefully, I became aware that I had denied an important part of myself—the opportunity to be a friend to my own father" (178–79).

This illustration was chosen largely because it is a fine example of introspection but also because it has bearing on Brian's case involving Bob. Goldberg was engaging in introspection throughout his session with Vincent and during his session with himself. He was looking into his own mind, assessing the feelings and reactions he found there in order to understand the effect that Vincent was having on him, especially in order to discover why Vincent's account of what had happened to his son was causing him so much uncharacteristic resentment. In the course of these introspections, he came to understand that his resentment stemmed from their similar experiences with their fathers. More pointedly, he felt that both sons had failed to understand, in their reproaches of their fathers for not allowing them to share their pain and to comfort them, that they had not paid any regard to their own failure to recognize that their fathers wanted their companionship but were unskilled in expressing this desire. Goldberg especially criticizes himself in this regard because he, as a psychoanalyst, should have been aware of his father's desire for friendship with his son. Thus, his introspections led to discoveries that were painful for him. At the same time, they enabled him to bring to some sort of closure his own struggle to discern the deeper secret that had been hidden from himself for the past year. That his work with Vincent began at roughly the same time as his father's death proved more than coincidental.

Introspectionism in American Psychology

Although Goldberg's Vincent case nicely illustrates the introspective process, this case is likely to evoke the following response from readers of this book: "But I am not a psychoanalyst. I am a pastor or a seminarian training to become a pastor. Is a pastor expected to engage in such deep and sustained self-analysis? Is anything useful to be gained from such self-analysis in the daily affairs of ministry?" To show that such introspection deserves a place in analyses of pastoral care experiences, we need to engage in a bit of history, first about American psychology, and second about pastoral care case writing. Before behaviorism burst on the scene in American psychology in the mid-1910s, the reigning paradigm in American psychology was introspectionism, a method of study largely transported to America from Germany. It had certain affinities with psychoanalysis, but it was viewed by American psychologists more as a research method than a therapeutic one. In recent years, the psychoanalyst Heinz Kohut has claimed the word for his particular version of psychoanalytic self psychology, and he views it, together with empathy, as the key element of the psychoanalytic process. For example, Kohut begins his *The Restoration of the Self* (1977) with the comment that "In comparison with my earlier contributions, the present work expresses more explicitly my reliance on the empathic-introspective stance, which has been defining my conceptual-theoretical outlook ever since 1959" (1977, xiii).

One of America's major proponents of introspectionism was William James, who described it in a section called "The Methods of Investigation" in his highly influential text *The Principles of Psychology*

(1950), first published in 1890. He states: "*Introspective observation is what we have to rely on first and foremost and always.* The word introspection need hardly be defined–it means, of course, the looking into our own minds and reporting what we there discover." Continuing, he notes that

> *Every one agrees that we there discover states of consciousness.* So far as I know, the existence of such states has never been doubted by any critic, however skeptical in other respects he may have been...All people unhesitatingly believe that they feel themselves thinking, and that they distinguish the mental state as an inward activity or passion, from all the objects with which it may cognitively deal. *I regard this belief as the most fundamental of all the postulates of Psychology.* (185)

James refuses to come down on either side of the question of whether introspection involves "feelings" or "thoughts," contending that this is a false distinction. To say that it focuses on "ideas" may give too strong a cognitive cast to it, so that, for example, Goldberg's awareness of his "resentment" toward Vincent might be screened out. To say that it involves only "feelings" or "emotions" may, however, obscure the fact that in introspection one is aware that a mental process is going on, as, for example, when Goldberg says that he had an "intuition" that Vincent was about to reveal a deep and painful secret.

James acknowledges that there has been considerable debate about the accuracy of introspective observation. What if one is self-deceived? Or what if an intentional decision to look at one's thoughts and feelings gets in the way of actually thinking or feeling them? He suggests, however, that the major objections to introspection as a method of investigation can be laid to rest if we recognize that it involves a two-step process. First, we have an immediate feeling or thought of which we are aware. Next, we report these and write about them, naming them, classifying and comparing them, and tracing their relations to other things: "While alive they are their own property; it is only *post-mortem* that they become his prey" (189). Thus, Goldberg initially has a very deep resentment toward Vincent of which he is very much aware, but whose meaning is not at all clear to him. As it continues to trouble and haunt him–Why am I feeling this way?–it becomes his prey, and he tries to identify its meaning. Initially, this effort was prompted by his desire to justify it, for it seemed incompatible with the fact that "this disturbed man was revealing his painful suffering." Goldberg considers these possibilities: Maybe it has to do with his own unresolved conflicts, and his resentment toward Vincent is related to these? Perhaps it involves some similarity he has with Vincent? Or does it relate in some way to Goldberg's own identification with Vincent's infant son? In any event, its context is the father-son relationship, and this proves an important clue to its meaning. The next day, his remembered poem begins to unlock the meanings of his unreasonable resentment, and by the end of the hour reserved for Vincent, he has cornered his prey. Key in this regard was seeing himself as the object of his father's resentment; in this, Vincent's treatment of his infant son had a previously unrecognized relevance to the resentment theme.

While it was during his session with himself that Goldberg cornered his prey, perhaps it was not until he wrote it all down in his chapter on "The Shameful Secret" that his introspective process assumed the underlying shape and form it came to have. As James indicates, when introspection is being employed as a research method, one usually writes it down. This helps to minimize the danger of self-deception and also allows the writer to return to it later and make additions and emendations.

In 1967, psychologist David Bakan (1967) wrote an essay arguing for the reinstatement of introspection in psychological science. Bakan noted that the rejection of the method of introspection is coincident with the inception of behaviorism in America. It was replaced because at the time it was considered an unreliable method of investigation. Far more reliable, it was believed, is the observation of external behavior, as this can be directly seen and verified by other observers. Bakan, however, felt that this criticism was greatly overblown. The unreliability of introspection can be counteracted by adhering to specified guidelines. Also, even if it has its problems, it is well worth trying to perfect it instead of jettisoning it, because the subject of introspections—what goes on in our minds—is the most interesting thing there is about humans. In addition, the history of behaviorism since John B. Watson first promulgated it (1970) has shown that the study of external behavior has its own difficulties. Bakan also questioned whether the rejection of introspection was even in the best interests of the behaviorist approach itself. Behaviorists should have recognized that what makes human behavior of interest to the researcher is not merely observable actions, but also what is going on inside, that is, what thoughts and feelings inform these actions.

An important problem, however, is the public nature of the report. While "the process of introspective observation is, in a sense, private, the information gleaned from the observations must be public" if they are to contribute to psychological science (Bakan, 1967, 99). The same point applies to the pastoral care case. Its public nature—the fact there are other readers besides the author—means that the author is likely to engage in some censorship of introspections for one or more reasons, such as not wanting others to know her thoughts and feelings about the parishioner, or her ministry as a profession or calling; judging that some of her thoughts and feelings are not sufficiently relevant to the case itself; or realizing that her deeper thoughts and feelings are unclear, or obscure, leading her to report only those that are more clear.

Bakan does not believe that the fact of its public nature is a fatal blow to introspection as a method of inquiry. To demonstrate this, he engaged in two separate "acts" of introspection, one in which he took as his subject the retention and revelation of secrets, the other involving the topic of suicide. He chose secrets because he felt that this was more amenable to introspection than to other methods of research, for by its very nature a secret is something that may not reflect itself in overt behavior. He chose suicide because he felt that this would enable him to "get inside" the mind of the person who actually contemplates and carries out the act of suicide. Thus, he was anticipating Heinz Kohut's view that psychoanalysis is an introspective-empathic process.

His introspections on suicide may have particular relevance to the pastoral care case, for they involved an effort to "step into" the mind of another. In other words, the issue was whether he could empathize with another individual by means of introspections into his own thoughts and feelings about the subject. In order to do this subject justice, he took an approach counter to the one he might have taken if he were merely engaging in conversation about the topic of suicide. That is, he did not begin with reasons why we should not commit suicide, nor with the question, Why commit suicide? but with the question, Why live? We will not reproduce all his reported introspections on the question, Why live? but will cite those that elicited a series of reflections about caretaking. Here is the paragraph that explores the relationship of suicide to caretaking:

The personality of the suicide, as has been pointed out many times, is one saturated with aggression, as though the liquid of aggression has been poured over every thought, feeling, and wish. But over and beyond this pervasive aggressive atmosphere, there seems to be a prototypic role, interiorized in the personality of the suicide, against which the act of aggression is turned. This role is best characterized by the term "caretaker." Somehow, it seems that the caretaker is much more diffuse than something we can ascribe to any person. I am tempted to say that in the act of suicide the person is aggressing against the mother, for the mother is the person who has kept the individual alive, who has taken him out of the danger of infantile impotence, and who "took care" of maintaining life until the individual was able to "take care" of himself. There is a sense in which the act of suicide is the undoing of the mother. Yet, although this may be true in part, it would seem that the caretaker is much more general and much more diffuse than can be ascribed to any person in the infantile family constellation. It is as though the individual who commits suicide is so bound by the caretaking function in the fulfillment of his wishes that he would rather slay the caretaker in himself than live the life of bondage to the caretaker. It would seem that the act of suicide is a spiteful act—whatever the psychodynamics of spite may be—against the tyrannical caretaker. In several of the cases to which the author exposed himself, he was able to pick up a sense of the subjects suffering the feeling of not being taken care of. The act of suicide is a single act, albeit a paradoxical one, in which the individual "takes care" of himself. (118–19)

Bakan implies that he would not have thought about the aggression in suicide being an attempt to "slay the caretaker" in oneself had he not engaged in this empathic act of introspection. Moreover, he discerns that one of the things inhibiting him from taking his own life is that his internalized "caretaker" is not so tyrannical. That is, he takes appropriate care of himself but not so intensely that he provokes a counteractive need to destroy himself. He acknowledges the difficulty of knowing how much he was able to set aside the fact that he knew he was engaging in a "pretense," that is, aware that he does not normally have suicidal thoughts. Even so, the exercise enabled him to gain insights into the minds of persons who seriously consider taking their own lives that he could not have gained in any other way. A key insight in this regard concerned the "internalized caretaker" thought. He recognized that he shared this characteristic with the suicidal person, but not to the degree that he needed to retaliate against it, as the suicidal person does.

The important point for our purposes here is that Bakan's introspections–his effort to explore his own thoughts and emotions about suicide–led to an increased understanding of those who commit or threaten to commit suicide. By looking inside his own mind, he understood the external situation much better. The point is not that he engaged in a "self-critical appraisal," for, after all, there was nothing to be self-critical about. (A failure to provide an actual suicidal person adequate assistance would, we assume, be a very different story.) Rather, he engaged in self-analysis, and this analysis of what came to mind when he thought about suicide led to an enhanced understanding of suicidal persons. Of course, this was a thought-experiment and not a case in real life. Yet it illustrates how we may enter into our own consciousness and describe in writing– in fact, clarify through writing–what we find there. This process, we suggest, does not normally occur in a sustained or systematic way in pastoral care case writing. Whether this is more because the pastoral care case format does not encourage it, or because the case writer does not know how to do it, is difficult to determine. Regardless, the case is limited, if not impoverished, as a result.

Why Is Introspection Absent from Pastoral Care Cases?

Little in the pastoral care case about the "situation" in the author's mind is remotely comparable to the attention the "situation" in the external world receives. Whether it *could* be incorporated into the case format is an open question, but a concluding section of "self-critical appraisal" falls far short of the sustained introspective engagement represented here by Goldberg and Bakan. Given Anton Boisen's own lifelong struggle with mental illness, we might have expected that the pastoral case writing would have taken a more introspective form. Our earlier quotation from his *The Exploration of the Inner World* (1936) suggests, however, that while he emphasized the student's need to learn to view the mentally ill empathically, he seems not to have recognized the value of introspection in this regard. Thus, he notes that

In the case of the mental sufferer...nothing can be taken for granted. His inner world has gone to pieces or it has been twisted out of shape. The culture patterns in which he was brought up no longer hold good and he questions everything. In so far, therefore, as we are to begin with his experiences and learn to see through his eyes, we must reexamine the foundations of all religious faith and learn to understand the laws and the forces which are involved in his experience. (252)

This is a fine statement of the need for empathy but says nothing about examining one's own mind to find evidence of an "inner world" that, from time to time and in its own way, "goes to pieces" or gets "twisted out of shape." Unless introspection accompanies empathy, empathy threatens to become mere sympathy, and the student views herself as being primarily in the "helping role."

This is not the place to engage in a psychobiography of Anton Boisen in order to discover the reasons why introspection did not play a larger role in his own development of pastoral case writing, but James E. Dittes has written a very provocative essay, "Boisen as Autobiographer" (1990), which sheds some light on the issue. This essay, based on Boisen's *Out of the Depths: An Autobiographical Study of Mental Disorders and Religious Experience* (1960), views Boisen's loss of sight in one eye at age seven as a sort of metaphor. Although Boisen downplayed the loss—"I have not been aware of the difference"—Dittes suggests that "monocular vision does make a difference: it deprives the person of the principal capacity for depth perception. The author's not noticing the difference illustrates the point" (225). It may also be noted that schizophrenia, the mental disorder with which Boisen was afflicted, typically manifests in attentional or perceptual distortions (e.g., another person's head seeming to expand then shrink) before becoming a full-fledged mental disorder (Claridge, 1995, 147–50).

Dittes goes on to explore Boisen's "lifelong infatuation—obsession, really—with Alice Batchelder," an unusual "love affair" (i.e., never consummated in marriage and characterized throughout by distance, both geographical and emotional) that the eighty-five-year-old Boisen insists on "taking at face value, as experienced, unprobed." He also notes that

Control was Boisen's prevailing strategy of life, and it has its limited success. His own brief evaluation of his "basic conflict" ("sexual hypersensitivity") is unremitting in the commitment of "self-discipline" at all costs. He administered to himself a kind of management therapy, pulling himself out of illness and stress by planning schedules, mapping terrain, devising agendas. As noted, his most effective work professionally was in his precise descriptive surveys. His programmatic efforts in developing chaplaincy staff and opportunities for students were an effective extension of this "agenda-therapy," which, however, repeatedly ran into problems when his followers wanted to use these opportunities to explore psychological depths Boisen was unready to pursue. So, indeed, is the autobiography itself, a descriptive marvel, charting, one after another, each event– once over all lightly–but without shading or nuance or interpretation or thematic connection. *Out of the Depths* maps, very candidly, the surface of the experience. (Dittes, 1990, 225)

For our purposes here, the key point is Boisen's commitment to "a kind of management therapy, pulling himself out of illness and stress by planning schedules, mapping terrain, devising agendas." Despite the fact that Boisen viewed himself as an heir of William James, whose *The Varieties of Religious Experience* attracted him as a seminary student at Union Seminary from 1908–1911 (Boisen, 1960, 60), this commitment to "management therapy" is more similar to Watson's behaviorism than to James's introspectionism, especially in Watson's view that "Personality is the sum of activities that can be discovered by actual observation of behavior over a long enough time to give reliable information. In other words, personality is but the end product of our habit systems" (Watson, 1970, 274).

During his first hospitalization in 1920–21, Boisen wrote a series of revealing letters to the psychiatrist who was the supervising physician on the ward to which he had been assigned, explaining that the men in his ward needed more recreational facilities and equipment. In one letter, he proposed a July 4th program involving baseball, relay races, and "special features," such as pillow fights, tug-of-war, and horseshoe pitching. Significantly in light of his visual problems, he asked for and received the assignment of hospital photographer. He reports that he took between six and seven hundred pictures of patients for the hospital records:

I was also authorized to take pictures of the buildings and grounds and activities. This was of course a most agreeable task, for the attractive grounds and the varied architecture of the buildings called for whatever skill and artistic sense a photographer might have. In the course of this assignment I undertook to make a complete survey of the hospital in pictures. I also completed a rough topographic map of the grounds. All these things kept me delightfully occupied, and provided me with an unusual opportunity to study the hospital. (Boisen, 1960, 136)

Clearly, he recognized the importance of patients' need for activity during their hospitalization for mental disorders, and he is justifiably proud of his early realization that such activity contributes to the maintenance, even improvement, of one's mental state. On the other hand, his description of his photographic work suggests that he was more concerned to explore the hospital grounds–its topography–than to probe the "inner world," either of the hospital or of his own mind. The very fact that he completed "a rough topographic map of the grounds" supports Dittes' point that he was more at home on the surface of mental life than in its depths.

Our purpose here is not to engage in a critique of Boisen himself, nor to minimize his positive contribution to the field of pastoral care. His reputation in this respect is secure. Rather, we are trying to account for the fact that pastoral case writing has been deficient in the opportunities it affords for systematic and sustained introspection. Like Boisen himself, it has served "agenda" and "management" interests, affording little opportunity for the kinds of introspective writing reflected in our excerpts from Goldberg and Bakan. To explain why this is a matter of practical concern, we will now return to the case presented in the preceding chapter. We will indicate how engagement in introspection would have made a difference in the way that Brian viewed Bob (more empathically), and in what the experience had to contribute to his own self-understanding, especially his sense of himself as a pastor. The following discussion is not intended to undermine in any way our earlier contention that the writing of this case had significant benefits for the author. Our intent is solely to make the case that even a very well-formulated and well-written case reveals the limitations of the pastoral care case as a pedagogical method or tool.

The Introspective Possibilities in the Case of the Contemporary Nicodemus

This discussion will necessarily focus on Brian, for the author is the one who would engage in systematic introspection. This does not mean, however, that we can simply ignore Bob, for the conversation between them is the experience that would serve as the catalyst for Brian's introspections, which we would then expect him to disclose, as fully as possible, in the pastoral care case itself. The fact that this conversation focuses on internal experience—Bob's desire for something "more" or "deeper" than he has experienced thus far in his life—makes this an especially good case for exploring the issue of introspection, because, as we have seen, introspection is primarily about what goes on in a person's mind. Brian addresses this in his comment early in the conversation when he says about his sermon, "Yeah, I guess I was saying that for most of us Presbyterians, myself included, our 'growing edge' might be a more careful nurturing of that internal experience of the close presence of God in our lives. We're good at *thinking about* God; sometimes we're not quite so good at *relating to* God." In other words, Brian implies that "relating" to God is an "internal experience," one that would involve "the close presence of God." Bob responds by saying that this is precisely what he feels he doesn't have and has never really had in his life. Brian follows up on Bob's comment with the request that he tell him "something about your spiritual journey so far."

What if, however, Brian had been looking at the matter from a more introspective point of view? Supposing he had posed this question: "I wonder what this 'internal experience' of 'the close presence' of God would feel like?" If "most of us Presbyterians" are better at "thinking about" God than "relating to" God (a claim he does not try to substantiate), this very admission might prompt him to wonder what it is like to "relate to" God. If a problem is something that has the form "I don't know my way about," we could say that he has just put his finger on a problem: We—you and I—do not know our way about when it comes to "relating to" God, to sensing the "close presence" of God. Stated this way, the problem that may then become the subject of introspection is not fundamentally different from Bakan's decision to introspect about secrets and suicide. Suppose that, after his conversation with Bob has concluded and before he writes his pastoral case (or even in the process of writing it), Brian were to write or type whatever comes into his mind about why "we" are not very good at relating to God, or about what it might be like to relate to God in a very personal manner. The latter, not unlike Bakan's introspections on suicide, might have a sort of "as-if" quality, but there is no reason in principle why Brian could not engage in introspection on this issue or problem. How would this introspection go? What would it reveal?

The author of this chapter (hereafter "I") actually did this. The process involved writing in a freely expressive way with pen and paper. The following is a faithful rendition of the combination of thoughts and feelings that resulted, with no attempt—at this juncture—to edit them. As I will indicate later, some editing would be appropriate when these introspections are integrated into the pastoral case itself. It should also be noted that during the process I was aware of associations to my own mother and father hovering, as it were, in the background. Unlike Goldberg, however, I did not concentrate on the meaning or significance of these associations, perhaps because I was aware that this was Brian's case, not my own. His own introspections would do well to take greater account of these personal associations, as they would likely—as in the case of Goldberg—have direct bearing on his counseling with Bob. In this sense, the following effort to introspect in Brian's place has an element of artificiality. It is useful, however, for illustrative purposes.

My first random thought was that we are not very good at relating to God because God is not very good at relating to us. I did not plan for my introspection to begin on what seems an accusatory note, that of holding God responsible in part for the absence of a close relationship. Yet there it was. This may or may not appear to others as a promising beginning, but it *is* a beginning, and it led to some further expression of resentment. The resentment centered on the fact that the problem always seems to be *our* problem, as though we are mainly at fault for the fact it exists.

This sense of resentment continued into some thoughts about how the onus is often put on the child to maintain good relations with mother and father, and I thought that Bob's question about being born again might (as in Goldberg's case) harbor deep feelings of resentment toward one or both of his parents. His observation that he feels "closer to God when we're in Maine" seemed relevant to this series of rather inchoate thoughts, as Maine was his birthplace. The fact that he asked Brian for an appointment on the basis of a sermon on Nicodemus' skepticism about entering our mother's womb a second time came into connection with the birthplace idea, and I began to wonder if Bob's resentment, if that is the name for it, was more related to his mother than his father. I also understood for the first time why one might view Bob as a skeptic, not because he doubted church doctrines, but because he, like Nicodemus, doubted he could return to the bliss of his original home in his mother's body.

This brought my thoughts back to Brian's comment that Bob could become emotionally moved while singing a Latin anthem. Two texts came to mind at that point. The first was William Styron's *Darkness Visible: A Memoir of Madness* (1990). In telling about what kept him from committing suicide the evening he had planned to do so, Styron relates that in a film he was watching on TV at the time, "the characters moved down the hallway of a music conservatory, beyond the walls of which, from unseen musicians, came a contralto voice, a sudden soaring passage from the Brahms *Alto Rhapsody*" (66). This sound, to which like all music—indeed, all pleasure—he had been numbly unresponsive for months,

> pierced my heart like a dagger, and in a flood of swift recollection I thought of all the joys the house had known: the children who had rushed through its rooms, the festivals, the love and work, the honestly earned slumber, the voices and the nimble commotion...All this I realized was more than I could ever abandon, even as what I had set out so deliberately to do was more than I could inflict on those memories, and upon those, so close to me, with whom the memories were bound. And just as powerfully I realized I could not commit this desecration on myself. I drew upon some last gleam of sanity to perceive the terrifying dimensions of the mortal predicament I had fallen into. I woke up my wife and soon telephone calls were made. The next day I was admitted to the hospital. (66–67)

Later, in describing his search for the origins of his illness, he offers the theory that the most significant factor "was the death of my mother when I was thirteen" and his sense that his had been a young person's "incomplete mourning," an inability "to achieve the catharsis of grief," leading him to carry within himself through later years "an insufferable burden of which rage and guilt, and not only dammed-up sorrow, are a part, and become the potential seeds of destruction" (79–80). How to account for his decision not to kill himself that evening? He believes his "own avoidance of death may have been belated homage to my mother. I do know that in those last hours before I rescued myself, when I listened to the passage from the *Alto Rhapsody*—which I'd heard her sing—she had been very much on my mind" (80). When I returned to this text later, words that were not recalled in the free expression period were "an insufferable burden of which rage and guilt, and not only dammed-up sorrow, are a part." This helped me to entertain the possibility that Bob's feeling of something "dammed-up inside of me" needing release had to do with his own incomplete mourning and that underlying his sorrow were feelings of rage and guilt.

My recollection of the Styron text led naturally to another text, Erik H. Erikson's *Young Man Luther* (1958). The passage that came to mind was Erikson's comment that "nobody could speak and sing as Luther later did if his mother's voice had not sung to him of some heaven" (72). Bob's faithfulness as a choir member, and his emotional response to music sung in Latin (indicating that sounds are more important than meanings) seemed related to his mother's caretaker role during infancy, when the sound of her voice was more important than her words, which were, after all, incomprehensible to him.

Other thoughts followed the mother/music associations. These were prompted by Brian's parenthetical comment—his "voice choking, eyes misting up with emotion"—which prefaced Bob's comment: "Sometimes when I am by myself in the woods, I just get overwhelmed with gratitude for the undeserved beauty of the world." While Bob goes on to talk about watching his grandchildren swimming in the lake and the sense of awe this evokes in him, my thoughts fixed on the phrase "Sometimes when I'm by myself in the woods," which called to mind Heinz Kohut's case of "Mr. X" in *The Restoration of the Self* (1977). Mr. X had alluded in the initial diagnostic interview to the "deep disappointment he had experienced concerning his father," but months later he recounted a daydream prompted by an account of his wanderings, on foot, through the wooded landscape of the beautiful region to which he had driven. What I recalled from the passage in Kohut's book was that the daydream involved Mr. X's earlier experience of walking through the woods with his father, and of being impressed by his father's ability to recall the names of birds. My association of Bob's experience to that of Mr. X led me to the thought that Bob's account of being alone in the woods, and feeling there a deep sense of gratitude for the undeserved beauty of the world, had something to do with his father, perhaps earlier experiences when he and his father walked the woods together. After the introspective period, when I took a closer look at the Styron text, it occurred to me that Bob might not have completed his mourning for his father. Was this, too, an element of his feeling "dammed-up inside"?

During the workshop discussion of Brian's case, I had asked Brian if his relationship to Bob might have a certain "father-son feel" to it, as though Bob cannot be close to his own sons and views Brian as a surrogate, or spiritual son. I reminded Brian of his statement that Bob "loves" his sermons and that *he* "loves" Bob because he needs all the fans he can get when faced with a skeptical audience. On the basis of this comment, it seemed that Bob meant more to Brian personally than Brian's "60-something" statement revealed. I don't recall that Brian responded to my query. Now, however, my introspections lead me to wonder why Brian needs to say that it is his sermons that Bob loves and why he speaks of his own love for Bob by classifying him among "the fans" a pastor can use when confronted by so much skepticism. Is there a love between the two men—as individuals—that Brian's language both disguises and reveals? If so, it might be that Brian's own introspections could begin precisely here. I would not presume to guess where these might lead, or what bearing they might have on his subsequent conversation with Bob, but they could be relevant to Bob's—and perhaps Brian's own—sense of feeling emotionally dammed-up inside.

While Brian recommended three good books for Bob to read, my introspections produced three texts as well—by Styron, Erikson, and Kohut. These came to mind, however, not for the purpose of giving Bob some reading to do, but to generate "hypotheses" about what Bob's problem was and how he could begin to find his way about in it. In other words, my introspections reveal that I did not take his *statement* of the problem at face value nor respond as if he had presented the problem in all of its fullness. His articulation of his problem in the terms the sermon set forth were only the starting point. Introspection was needed for me to find my own way about, for, in effect, Bob had created a problem for me. I needed to clear the fog in which I found myself when he began to present his reasons for making an appointment to see his pastor.

If these introspections had found their way into Brian's pastoral case report, no doubt they would have required editing. Their primary value for the pastoral care case itself, however, is that they guided me toward an association of Bob's love for the woods and his relationship to his father, a hypothesis that would need to be confirmed—or disconfirmed—through further conversation with Bob. Conversely, the analysis that Styron offers in his discussion of "incomplete mourning," especially his view that not only sorrow but also rage and guilt are present when mourning has not been completed, might also be highlighted. Has Bob also suffered the death of his mother? Is Bob holding inside himself not only sorrow but also rage and guilt in connection to his mother? Is Brian, having recently left the city in which he was reared, experiencing a similar mourning, one also associated with the emotional loss of his mother? Are both men responding, in effect, to the emotional subtext of the gospel account of Nicodemus, who wonders if there is any form of rebirth that could begin to approximate the experience of entering one's mother's womb a second time?

If Bob's (and Brian's) problem is one of incomplete mourning, this could mean, in effect, that Brian would view this case as one of "grief counseling." Although he might inquire into whether Bob's parents are actually dead or not, the fact of their physical deaths would be far less important than Bob's experience at some point in his life of their "emotional deaths" for him. Based on my experience of men, and exactly reversing my introspective process, I might (if I were in Brian's place) begin by centering on Bob's relationship to his father, as it is likely to be easier, less threatening, for him to talk about his father than his mother. The association between his emotional response to the singing of Latin anthems and the loss of his mother would always, however, be near the center of my thoughts; for this, I would suppose, is a key insight into the causes and sources of his current loneliness. Nicodemus' question—"Can a man enter his mother's womb a second time?"—is at the heart of both skepticism and a man's deepest unconscious desires. Spiritual rebirth is then a secondary desire that comes to mind when the former wish is known to be foreclosed.

Possible Objections to Introspection

One possible objection to the foregoing approach to the pastoral care case is that it seems to move an ordinary pastoral care case in a psychotherapeutic direction. We do not, however, wish to create the impression that introspection is a psychotherapeutic form of pastoral counseling in disguise. Rather, our concern is to make a case for the place of introspection in the development of a pastoral care case. As noted earlier, this introspection might occur in the interim between the pastoral encounter and the writing of the case. For some, it may best be carried out as a thought process first, and then set down on paper. For others, the introspective process and writing are essentially one and the same. For still others, there may be a combination of thought process and random note-taking. How much time one devotes to it cannot be legislated in advance. Much more important than the time involved is to set aside the tendency to begin immediately thinking in terms of how to help Bob with his problem. Brian needs to find his way about, not only situationally but also personally, and the way to do this, we suggest, is to engage in self-analysis aided by the process of introspection. Since we are not Brian, we could only guess at where this process would take him. (To illustrate the process, we *have*, however, shown how one of us, assuming the role of Brian, employed the introspective process to find his way about in Brian's own pastoral case.) Our point is that Brian will have difficulty finding his way about in the situation that Bob represents if he has not found his way about in his own thoughts and emotions, as these have been elicited by Bob's problem.

This is not, then, an appeal for Brian to adopt the psycho-therapeutic role. Quite possibly, he does too much of this already with his "history taking" approach: "Maybe you could start by telling me what you heard me saying in the sermon" and "Could you tell me something about your spiritual journey so far?"—as if to suggest that when all the relevant facts are known, he will then be in a position to offer his diagnosis. The introspective process may well suggest a move in the opposite direction, for example, the proposal that they meet next time in Bob's favorite restaurant and carry on their conversation over a meal. As Brian himself acknowledged, while Presbyterians may be good at thinking about God, they're not quite as good at relating to God. Perhaps the first step toward addressing this problem is to get better at relating to each other. Having a leisurely meal together is a place to begin. Since Bob is now retired, this could be a welcome activity for a man who spent his working days in the company of many others. If Brian and Bob were to abandon the office and its formality and instead have an occasional lunch together—regardless of what they talk about—this might enable both men to feel more at home in the worlds where they currently find themselves. Then, perhaps, the two men might find truth in Brian's view that becoming born again is a process, one that occurs gradually over the course of weeks and months as two men open their minds and hearts to each other.

Could introspection be assimilated into the pastoral care case? Could it become part of its structure or format? If done in some formal manner, such as by adding a section called "introspection," we worry that it would be drawn into the same "agenda" and "managing" tendency that we saw in Boisen. We do, however, advocate the method of introspection itself. In chapter 1, we saw that note-writing played a major role in the development of the pastoral case method. William James and other advocates of introspection understood the value of note-writing to the introspective process, as this practice enabled the writer to create some order out of the inchoate thoughts and feelings that were jostling around in his or her mind. It may be that the pastoral care case should be supplemented by another form–"introspective note-taking"–in order to maximize its benefits to the pastor and those with whom the pastor engages in caring ministry. It may be that the atrophy of pastoral care to which we refer in chapter 3 might thereby be at least partially reversed. We noted at the conclusion of this chapter that many churches are "forging unto unknown territory." Perhaps the most unknown of all such territories is the human mind, the exploration of which may enable us to perceive the deep commonalities between its confusions and clarities and the complex interhuman relationships that comprise the living experience of local congregations.

Epilogue:
Becoming a Local Religious Author

Throughout the educational process, from preschool through seminary, a future pastor will have been introduced to many texts written by others. As children, we learned to read before we were taught to write. As we grew older, writing became a larger part of our education, and in college and seminary we were required to write papers as a condition of passing our courses. Yet we were always aware that our own writings paled in comparison with those of the authors we were required to read. Our own writings were, in fact, mostly discussions of what someone else had written.

We have advanced in this book the rather bold proposal that in writing a pastoral care case, one not only becomes an author in one's own right but also becomes a *religious* author. In chapter 2, we set forth several reasons why the writer of a pastoral care case is a religious author. These points need not be repeated here. As we bring this book to a conclusion, however, we feel we should say something about why we believe that pastors *should* view themselves as religious authors. Most pastors continue to view themselves as readers, not authors, and they may not even dare to consider themselves authors until they become involved in writing theses for their Doctor of Ministry degrees, or, at retirement, give serious thought to writing about their pastoral experiences. Even when they are engaged in writing sermons, they do not think about themselves as religious authors, though in fact they clearly are.

Why is this the case? Why is it that pastors do not consider themselves religious authors? Could this be because we tend to view authors as writing for a readership that is, by definition, "nonlocal"? If a text is designed for a larger audience, authorship is claimed for

155

it, even if the larger audience is relatively small, such as books written in a very specialized field of research. Conversely, if one is writing about local matters, for a local readership, we do not ascribe to this person true "authorial" status. If, for example, a citizen writes a letter to the editor of a local newspaper about a local problem (the noise caused by leaf blowers or the incompetence of the local school board), we tend not to credit the letter writer with being an author. On the other hand, his next-door neighbor who writes children's stories for a wider public is considered an author because her books are distributed and read outside the local community. Our uncertainty about whether to ascribe authorial status to a person who has written a family history for distribution to relatives, or a person who has written the history of a local church for distribution to church members, makes our point.

The original authors in the religious movement we now call Christianity were, however, *local* religious authors. Paul's letters to the various communities he had been involved in developing are obvious examples of this. They are all addressed to a local constituency. So, too, with the gospels. Matthew wrote his gospel for "the Matthean community." The fact that scholars dispute where this community was located and whom it comprised does not challenge—rather, it supports and confirms—the fact that Matthew wrote for a local readership. In time, of course, Paul's letters were circulated to readers who had no direct knowledge about the local circumstances addressed in the letter, and biblical scholars today give a great deal of attention to the task of reconstructing these circumstances. But they were originally written for a local readership, and Paul was a local religious author. That he was local, however, does nothing to detract from his importance as a religious author.

Two decades ago, Wade Clark Roof, an ordained minister and a sociologist of religion, developed a local-cosmopolitan theory of religious commitment (1978). He argued that in modern secular society, one important sphere that continues to provide support for traditional religion is the local community. Thus, local community attachment is a primary source of religious commitment. He also suggested that this attachment varies on a local-cosmopolitan continuum that assesses the extent to which individuals are oriented toward their immediate social environment as opposed to the broader society. He noted that "locals are more attached to their immediate social locale and are quite sensitive to the primary groups with which they interact, such as the family, neighborhood cliques, and community organizations. In contrast, cosmopolitans have their commitments centered outside the residential community and tend to identify more with abstract, generalized groups that may be spatially remote" (41). Cosmopolitans have broader social perspectives, while those of locals tend to be more narrowly focused.

Throughout the history of Christianity, localism and cosmopolitanism have coexisted in an uneasy though sometimes creative tension. This tension has flared up in controversies within denominations and even within individual congregations. Individuals—pastors and laity—often experience this tension within themselves, as their "localistic" and "cosmopolitan" loyalties sometimes clash. There is no easy way to reconcile these two forms or types of religious commitment, and we will probably never see the day when those who are primarily local-oriented and those who are mainly cosmopolitan-oriented will fully recognize the validity of the perspective that is not their own. Often, we define ourselves over against the other orientation in spite of the fact that, in Roof's view, they actually reflect a continuum.

The pastoral care case, however, is inevitably tilted toward the localistic orientation. Its particular strength as a form of religious authorship is that it exhibits sensitivity to the primary groups in which Christians interact on a regular basis with one another and with the community. Although it may therefore seem that localism is stronger in small towns, where people are more likely to know one another by name, the localism-cosmopolitanism continuum is not synonymous with the small town–large city distinction. Some of the most localistic expressions of religious commitment are found in cities, orthodox Jews being a notable example. In a study of members of a Mennonite congregation in a large city, Joseph Smucker (1986) found that, while the "community" they experienced in the city congregation had different attributes from the rural communities in which they had grown up, they identified themselves as a close-knit group with strong localistic loyalties. As one member put it, "I feed on the Christian support, on the open sharing. It's like an extended family." In some ways, their localistic orientation was strengthened, more deeply internalized, as they adopted the broader perspectives of a religiously cosmopolitan outlook, and this was reflected in their involvement in service-oriented jobs and professions.

Thus, the pastoral care case is the work of a *local* religious author. She may be no less cosmopolitan in outlook than those who write about "abstract, generalized groups that may be spatially remote," but when assuming the role of religious author, she privileges the local context and localistic attachments and commitments. In the world of the pastoral care case, it is always local time.

Consider, for example, the case of Jonathan Edwards, often claimed to be America's greatest theologian. We rarely think of this important theologian of the Christian church as a local pastor, nor are we very much aware of the fact that he faced continual challenges to his congregational leadership. A brief illustration will show, however, that his ministry eventually came to grief over an incident that centered around very localistic attachments (i.e., primary groups).

Edwards had served the Congregational church in Northampton, Massachusetts, first as assistant pastor, then as pastor, for seventeen years. He had already weathered several difficult situations, including a backlash against the spiritual awakening he had been promoting, when several persons influenced by what he and others were preaching committed suicide. The incident that concerns us here involved several boys who had gotten hold of a book of instructions for midwives and were passing it around to other teenagers. Some of the teenagers were from the town's better families who were members of the church. When Edwards learned of the situation, he informed the congregation after a regular service of what had been going on, and he asked it to authorize an investigation. When this authorization was given, he read a list of the names of young people who were to appear at the investigation, but he failed to make a distinction between those who were accused and those who were being called as witnesses. This failure to differentiate the accused from the witnesses upset many of the parents because some of their own children's names were on the list.

The investigation continued for two months with twenty-two witnesses implicating eleven teenagers. Finally, two boys confessed to contemptuous behavior against the authority of the church, and this closed the investigation. However, ill feeling toward Edwards continued to simmer. Church members asked such questions as, Was this a private matter and not the minister's business? Was there a limit to the church's interference in matters of personal conduct? Does pastoral authority take precedence over parental authority in the disciplining of children? In addition to these quite legitimate questions, more emotional issues were involved. A major one was that Jonathan's wife, Sarah, and some of the Edwards' children testified against the children of parishioners. Even though only two boys from the total of eleven accused were actually charged with wrongdoing, the fact that the names of others were brought into the investigation by the minister's wife and children did not set well with the parishioners involved. Thus, Edwards' own failure to distinguish between the accused and the witnesses was now compounded by his family's involvement in the accusations.

Edwards discussed the controversy over his handling of the problem with his father, who had recently withheld communion from the entire congregation in East Windsor because of a dispute over his refusal to baptize the child of a couple who had failed to secure the consent of the bride's parents before marrying. The result of this father-son discussion is not known. What *is* known is that Edwards continued to preach about young people's neglect of religion. However, where his efforts ten years earlier to create a religious sensitivity in the youth had contributed to the spiritual awakening, this time his warnings fell on deaf ears. Resentment among church members toward Edwards over the "bad book" investigation was deep. It became clear that his ministry in Northampton could no longer be effective, but the contention and hostility continued for another six years before the congregation succeeded in dismissing him from his position (a small number of members, his loyal supporters, had blocked these efforts). His ministry there had lasted twenty-three years, but during the last several years of his Northampton pastorate, he spent much of his time writing the theology that was later to gain him the reputation of being America's greatest theologian, securing him a place in cosmopolitan Christianity. The "bad book" episode, being so local, has long since been forgotten. Yet the issues that were raised in this dispute about what is private and what is public, and about parental versus religious authority, were local expressions of the cosmopolitan issues that were troubling the nation at the time.

Of course, Edwards did not develop this incident into a pastoral care case. "The Bad Book Case and How I Seem to Have Mishandled It" does not appear anywhere in his rather voluminous writings. Instead, the controversy became the occasion for him to retreat to his study to concentrate on his theological authorship. But what if he *had* felt that this very incident was worthy of his best authorial skills, and what if he *had* brought his theological acumen, his powers of social analysis, his psychological perceptiveness, and his own introspection to bear on this critical incident? What if he had chosen to become a truly *local* religious author, one who was willing to explore the primary group attachments and commitments involved in order to understand what went wrong, how it could have been handled differently, and even how he might be able to redeem the situation, however bleak it appeared? Would his ministry at Northampton have turned out differently if he had chosen to write a pastoral care case as discussed in this book? In our view, it *would* have made a significant difference in his own ministry and, perhaps even more importantly, in privileging the local. It would have served as a model for writing theologically.

When Edwards entered his study and closed the door behind him so that he could write his theology undisturbed, he took a fateful step away from the localistic orientation that is so much a part of the gospels and of the epistles of Paul. The pastoral care case model presented in this book has its roots in the convergence—evident in the New Testament itself—of the healing stories of Jesus the villager and the congregational struggles of Paul the urbanite. Thus, we invite the field of pastoral care to turn the clock back, for the pastoral care cases we write and share with others are grounded in the very origins of the Christian religion, in a place where it is always local time.

You too can be a religious author. We invite you to begin where you are and to write about what you know from direct, firsthand experience. Think of yourself less as a novelist faced with the daunting task of creating a full narrative of your tenure at Second Presbyterian Church (or wherever you happen to be), and more as a poet who is attuned to the discrete events of daily life, the episodes that do not add up, that are ill-fitting, unmanageable, even downright chaotic. Many of these episodes are ones in which care was called for and in which care, in one fashion or another, was provided. These are rarely, if ever, headline events, but they are the very stuff— and staff—of our life together.

Let no one disparage these episodes—episodes of ordinary trial, trouble, and tribulation—or dismiss the acts of kindness, of thoughtfulness, and of simple, unassuming love that they engender or inspire. And, as we contemplate these episodes of need and fallible response, let us not forget to write of those in which *we* were ministered to, when others saw our own neediness and enabled us to experience a solidarity with Jesus from which we, in our consuming need to care for others, had become estranged. We too easily think of care giving and care receiving as fixed traits adhering to persons. Instead, they are responses in situations of need, and no one of us is a stranger to the experience of discovering that what we thought to be an act of caring for another was one in which we were the real recipient of care. This is what it means to stand together in solidarity with Jesus. To be a local religious author is to testify to this solidarity. Blest be this tie that binds our hearts in Christian love, and blest be those who take time to write and reflect on their own local versions of it.

References

Asquith, Glenn H., Jr. (1980). "The Case Study Method of Anton T. Boisen." *The Journal of Pastoral Care* 34: 84–94.

—— (1990). "An Experiential Theology." In *Turning Points in Pastoral Care: The Legacy of Anton Boisen and Seward Hiltner*, edited by L. Aden and J. H. Ellens. Grand Rapids: Baker Book House, 19–31.

Bakan, David (1967). *On Method: Toward a Reconstruction of Psychological Investigation.* San Francisco: Jossey-Bass.

Balswick, J. (1990). "Social Sciences." In *Dictionary of Pastoral Care and Counseling*, edited by Rodney J. Hunter et al. Nashville: Abingdon Press.

Boisen, Anton Theophilus (1936). *The Exploration of the Inner World.* New York: Harper and Brothers.

—— (1960). *Out of the Depths: An Autobiographical Study of Mental Disorder and Religious Experience.* New York: Harper and Brothers.

Cabot, Richard C. (1906). *Case Teaching in Medicine: A Series of Graduated Exercises in the Differential Diagnosis, Prognosis and Treatment of Actual Cases of Disease.* Boston: D. C. Heath and Co.

—— (1911, rev. 1915). *Differential Diagnosis.* 2 vols. Philadelphia: Saunders.

Cabot, Richard C., and Russell L. Dicks (1936). *The Art of Ministering to the Sick.* New York: Macmillan.

Capps, Donald (1984). *Pastoral Care and Hermeneutics.* Philadelphia: Fortress Press.

Claridge, Gordon (1995). *Origins of Mental Illness: Temperament, Deviance and Disorder.* Cambridge, Mass.: Mallor Books.

Cryer, Newman S., Jr., and John M. Vayhinger, eds. (1962). *Casebook in Pastoral Counseling.* New York: Abingdon Press. (Orig. ed. 1952.)

Dicks, Russell L. (1939). *And Ye Visited Me: Source Book for Ministers in Work with the Sick.* New York: Harper and Brothers.

—— (1944, rev. 1949). *Pastoral Work and Personal Counseling.* New York: Macmillan.

Dittes, James E. (1990). "Boisen as Autobiographer." In *Turning Points in Pastoral Care: the Legacy of Anton Boisen and Seward Hiltner,* edited by L. Aden and J. H. Ellens. Grand Rapids: Baker Book House.

—— (1999). *Re-Calling Ministry,* edited by Donald Capps. St. Louis: Chalice Press.

Drakeford, John W. (1959). "Ways to Learn Pastoral Counseling." In *An Introduction to Pastoral Counseling,* edited by Wayne E. Oates. Nashville: Broadman Press.

Emerson, Ralph Waldo (1983). "An Address to the Senior Class in Divinity College, Cambridge." In *Essays and Lectures.* New York: The Library of America.

Erikson, Erik H. (1958). *Young Man Luther: A Study in Psychoanalysis and History.* New York: W. W. Norton.

Farley, Edward (1996). *Deep Symbols: Their Postmodern Effacement and Reclamation.* Valley Forge, Pa.: Trinity Press International.

Freud, Sigmund (1955). "The 'Uncanny'." In *The Standard Edition of the Complete Psychological Works of Sigmund Freud,* edited by J. Strachey, 218–56. Vol. 17. London: Hogarth Press.

—— (1959). *Group Psychology and the Analysis of the Ego.* Translated and edited by J. Strachey. New York: W. W. Norton. (Orig. Eng. trans., New York: Boni and Liveright, 1920.)

Gadamer, Hans-Georg (1975). *Truth and Method.* New York: Crossroad.

Gerkin, Charles V. (1986). *Widening the Horizons: Pastoral Responses to a Fragmented Society.* Philadelphia: Westminster Press.

—— (1997). *An Introduction to Pastoral Care.* Nashville: Abingdon Press.

Gladden, Washington (1898). *The Christian Pastor and the Working Church.* New York: Charles Scribner's Sons.

Goldberg, Carl (1991). *Understanding Shame.* Northvale, N.J.: Jason Aronson.

Gorsuch, Nancy J. (1999). *Pastoral Visitation.* Minneapolis: Fortress Press.

Graham, Larry Kent (1992). *Care of Persons, Care of Worlds.* Nashville: Abingdon Press.

Hall, Charles E. (1992). *Head and Heart: The Story of the Clinical Pastoral Education Movement.* Decatur, Ga.: Journal of Pastoral Care Publications.

Halperin, David J. (1993). *Seeking Ezekiel: Text and Psychology.* University Park: Pennsylvania State University Press.

Hiltner, Seward (1949). *Pastoral Counseling.* Nashville: Abingdon Press.

—— (1952). *The Counselor in Counseling: Case Notes in Pastoral Counseling.* Nashville: Abingdon Press. (Orig. ed. 1950.)

—— (1958). *Preface to Pastoral Theology.* Nashville: Abingdon Press.

—— (1980). "A Descriptive Appraisal, 1935–1980." *Pastoral Psychology* 29:86–98.

——, ed. (1945). *Clinical Pastoral Training.* Commission on Religion and Health, Federal Council of the Churches of Christ in America.

Hunter, Rodney. J. (1990). A Perspectival Pastoral Theology. In *Turning Points in Pastoral Care: The Legacy of Anton Boisen and Seward Hiltner,* edited by L. Aden and J. H. Ellens. Grand Rapids: Baker Book House, 53–79.

James, William (1950). *The Principles of Psychology.* Vol. 1. New York: Dover Publications.

—— (1982). *The Varieties of Religious Experience.* New York: Penguin Books.

Johnson, Paul E. (1953). *Psychology of Pastoral Care.* Nashville: Abingdon Press.

Kohut, Heinz (1977). *The Restoration of the Self.* New York: International Universities Press.

Langdell, Christopher Columbus (1871). *A Selection of Cases on the Law of Contracts: With References and Citations, Prepared for Use as a Text-Book in Harvard Law School.* Boston: Little, Brown, and Company.

Levinson, Daniel J., et al (1978). *The Seasons of a Man's Life.* New York: Alfred A. Knopf.

McFague, Sallie (1997). *Super, Natural Christians: How We Should Love Nature.* Minneapolis: Fortress Press.

Meyer, Leonard B. (1956). *Emotion and Meaning in Music.* Chicago: University of Chicago Press.

Nouwen, Henri J. M. (1968). "Anton T. Boisen and Theology Through Living Human Documents." *The Journal of Pastoral Care* 19:49–63.

—— (1977). "Boisen and the Case Study Method." *The Chicago Theological Seminary Register* 67:12–32.

Petermann, Bruno (1932). *The Gestalt Theory and the Problem of Configuration.* London: Kegan Paul, Trench, Trubner.

Redlich, Joseph (1914). *The Common Law and the Case Method in American University Law Schools: A Report to the Carnegie Foundation for the Advancement of Teaching.* Bulletin no. 8. New York: D. B. Updike; Boston: Merrymount Press.

Ricoeur, Paul (1976). *Interpretation Theory: Discourse and the Surplus of Meaning.* Fort Worth: Texas Christian University Press.

—— (1979). "Naming God." *Union Seminary Quarterly Review* 34:220.

—— (1980). "Toward a Hermeneutic of the Idea of Revelation." In *Essays on Biblical Interpretation,* edited by L. S. Mudge. Philadelphia: Fortress Press, 77–81.

—— (1981). *Hermeneutics and the Human Sciences.* Edited and translated by John B. Thompson. Cambridge: Cambridge University Press.

Roof, Wade Clark (1978). *Community and Commitment: Religious Plausibility in a Liberal Protestant Church.* New York: Elsevier.

Smucker, Joseph (1986). "Religious Community and Individualism: Conceptual Adaptations by One Group of Mennonites." *Journal for the Scientific Study of Religion* 25: 273–91.

Snyder, William U. (1947). *Casebook of Non-Directive Counseling.* Boston: Houghton Mifflin.

SteinhoffSmith, Roy Herndon (1999). *The Mutuality of Care.* St. Louis: Chalice Press.

Styron, William (1990). *Darkness Visible: A Memoir of Madness.* New York: Random House.

Thornton, Edward E. (1970). *Professional Education for Ministry: A History of Clinical Pastoral Education.* Nashville: Abingdon Press.

Tillich, Paul (1963). *Systematic Theology.* Vol. 3. Chicago: The University of Chicago Press.

Valdes, Mario J., ed. (1991). *A Ricoeur Reader.* Toronto: University of Toronto Press.

Watson, John B. (1970). *Behaviorism.* New York: W. W. Norton.

Wiesel, Elie (1969). *Night.* Translated by S. Rodway. New York: Avon Books.

Wise, Carroll A. (1951). *Pastoral Counseling: Its Theory and Practice.* New York: Harper & Brothers.

Wittgenstein, Ludwig (1958). *Philosophical Investigations.* 3d ed. Translated by G. E. M. Anscombe. New York: Macmillan.

Index

appropriation, in pastoral care case interpretation, 78–80; illustration of, 99–103

Bakan, David, 140–43

Boisen, Anton, and mentally ill, 11; use of case method, 12; case format, 12–13; theology of, 12–13; and spiritual healing, 20; influence on Hiltner, 22; and introspection, 143–46

Cabot, Richard, and case method, 10–11, 13; and note–writing, 15–18; and work of minister, 20

case format, in psychiatric setting, 12–13; in general hospital, 14; in pastoral care case, 43–50

case interpretation, procedure for, 6–11; medical model of, 10–11; in pastoral care case, 53–57; as series of readings, 78–80. *See also* self–interpretation

case method of teaching, 5–6; in clinical pastoral training, 11–14

christological values, in pastoral care, 66–68; in pastoral care case, 91–98

congregation, and case method, 1–2; in pastoral care case, 47–59; caring role of, 58–59; controversy in, 158–60

cosmopolitanism, 156–58

cure of souls, demise of term, 19–20, 72

deductive reasoning, 8–9

diagnostic reasoning, 10–11, 13

Dicks, Russell, and note-writing, 14–18; collaboration with Cabot, 15–17; and creation of pastoral care and counseling model, 20

Dittes, James E., on Boisen as autobiographer, 144–46

Dunbar, Helen Flanders, and creation of case format, 12

eductive method, Hiltner's advocacy of, 23, 25

Edwards, Jonathan, and the bad-book episode, 158–60

Emerson, Ralph Waldo, 112, 120–21, 124, 130

facts, in legal cases, 6; in pastoral care cases, 57–62; evaluation of, 64–71

Fairbanks, Rollin, contribution to note-writing method, 15

Farley, Edward, 66, 72–74

format, of Boisen's psychiatric case model, 12–13; of Cabot and Dicks's note-writing model, 15–17; of pastoral care case model, 43–50. *See also* pastoral care case

formfulness, of ministry experiences, 109

Freud, Sigmund, 67